STEAM

LOCOMOTIVES

Pages 2-3
The joining of the Union Pacific and Central
Pacific Railroads in Utah, 1869.
Pages 4-5
A McConnell 2-2-2 'Large Bloomer'.

F. George Kay

STEAM LOCOMOTIVES

Galahad Books   New York

625.26

Published by
Galahad Books, a division of A & W Promotional Book Corporation,
95 Madison Avenue, New York, N.Y. 10016

Library of Congress Catalog Card No: 74-75138
ISBN: 0-88365-231-5

Copyright © 1974 The Hamlyn Publishing Group Limited

Manufactured in Great Britain

CONTENTS

FOREWORD

Industrial and social history is my profession; the steam locomotive is my recreational interest. Occupation and hobby are allied, for the railway engine brought with it a bloodless revolution which spread from the pitheads of northern England to every corner of the world. The steam locomotive's birth, life, and death spanned fewer than 150 years; its impact will remain as long as our industrial civilization exists.

In these pages I have confined myself to the mainstream of the locomotive story. Inevitably, some fascinating developments for specialized purposes have been omitted for reasons of space and in order to provide what I hope is a factual and coherent narrative.

No comparable invention has ever aroused such literary enthusiasm as the steam locomotive. Contemporary works preserved by the British Museum, the Patent Office and the London Library have been con-

sulted as often as possible. Noteworthy were *Life of George Stephenson,* Samuel Smiles (1857); *Who Invented the Locomotive Engine?,* O. D. Hedley (1858); *Railway Locomotives,* D. K. Clark (1861); *The Locomotive Engine,* C. E. Stretton (1894), and the files of *Locomotive Magazine, Railway Magazine,* and *Railway Gazette.* In addition, BTC historical records and the house journals of the railway companies were an inexhaustible source of data published at the time of the locomotives concerned. I must also mention the exhibits and records of the Science Museum and the museums in the railway towns of Britain, and the railway preservation societies which are ensuring that the steam locomotive shall be immortal in reality as well as memory.

Modern works consulted include *A Century of Locomotive Building,* I. G. H. Warren (1923); *Ein Jahrhundert Eisenbahn,* Friedrich Lohse (1923); *The Book*

below **Passenger trains on the Liverpool and Manchester Railway in 1831. First class carriages (top) were replicas of the stage coaches running on the turnpikes, even to the extent of giving each coach a name. At the rear is a mail coach; mails were first carried by train in 1830. Second class passengers (lower illustration) travelled in open trucks, often, as at the rear, without seats. In the mid 1830s awnings were added.**

of the Locomotive, G. G. Jackson (1924); commemorative literature of the Baltimore 'Fair of the Iron Horse' (1927); *One Hundred Years of American Railroading,* John W. Starr Jnr (1928); *Land Transport: Railway Locomotives* HMSO (1948); *The Railways of Britain, Past and Present,* O. S. Nock (1948); *L'ère du Rail,* L. M. Jouffray (1953).

Finally, no writer on railways can fail to be influenced and stimulated by that doyen of railway historians, Hamilton Ellis, whose erudition is embellished with humour and affection. His classic *British Railway History, 1830–1876 and 1877–1947* (2 vols 1954 and 1959) has been invaluable.

F. George Kay

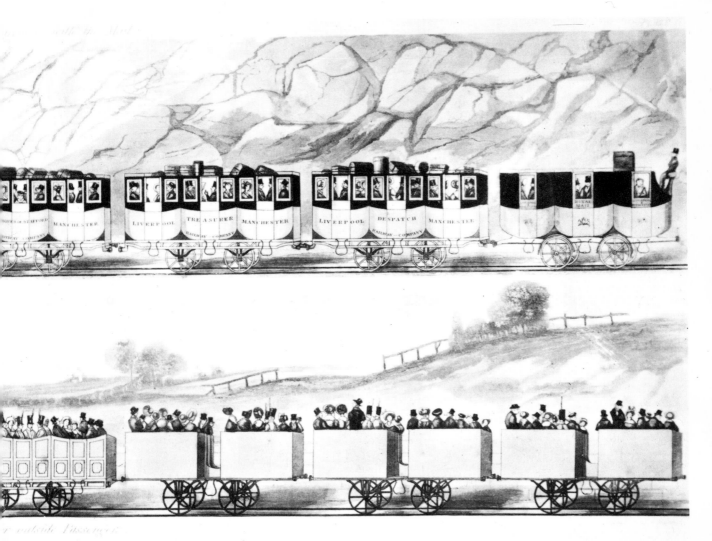

BIRTH OF AN IDEA

The invention and improvement of the steam locomotive were both necessary and inevitable. England, as the leading industrial nation, was developing a complex system of mass production in factories, requiring transport of raw materials and manufactures. Carriage by sea and inland water solved some of the problems. The early prosperity of the Midlands was partly due to the proximity of the river Severn, known from medieval times as the King's High Stream. Navigable canals and rivers made East Anglia prosperous and highly populated prior to the industrial revolution.

However, vital raw materials–iron ore and coal–were all too often far from natural waterways. New canals helped to ease the difficulties, but the barges were slow, and canal construction in hilly areas costly or impracticable. Roads were mostly in appalling condition, and in the mid-eighteenth century the majority of freight wagons had tyres of at least 9 inches width in order to avoid sinking to the axles. They were hauled by horses or oxen at 2 to 3 mph. Passengers and mails had the benefit of the turnpikes, on which heavy tolls had to be paid, and the price of speed was prohibitive. Mail coaches required a horse for every mile of the route–four horses for a stage of 10 to 12 miles to be covered in an hour, and the reserves in case of injury or bad conditions.

To transport raw materials from port or mine to factory, long trains of packhorses had often to be used, as in the case of Cornish clay for Midland potteries. Processed materials–textiles, china, metal goods–left the factories in the same way. Commerce was dependent on transport which rarely moved at more than 3 mph and a load was largely restricted to the maximum a horse could drag or carry.

Nevertheless at the mines and in many of the newly-built factories steam power was revolutionizing the means of production. All that remained was to adapt the machinery as a self-propelling power plant. However, the practical problems of doing so were enormous. The steam engines used for pumping and powering machines were of the low pressure condensing type, heavy and bulky in relation to their power output. Much higher steam pressure and more efficient use of it were essential, and that meant major improvements in metallurgy and engineering skill.

Some inventors were content to demonstrate that steam could provide mobility without showing much concern about the danger of comparatively high pressure steam in a fragile boiler, or the dubious benefits of a machine which could merely move itself around. Nicolas James Cugnot, a French artillery officer, built a three-wheeled engine in 1769, and demonstrated it to the Ministry of War on a piece of waste ground in Paris. The vertical bronze cylinders slowly turned the rear wheels and for ten minutes the machine lumbered forward before colliding with a wall and fracturing the steam joints. Cugnot's intention was that his engine

G. MORTON, Del.

The Guide or Engineer is seated in front, having a lever rod from the hind part of the Coach contains the machinery for producing the Steam, contains about 60 Gallons of water, is placed under the body of the Coach produced will be dispelled by the action of the Vehicle ___ At different sta travelling is intended to be from 8 to 10 miles per hour.___ The present Steam Ca

Horse-drawn road coaches carrying the mails could average 10 mph at the dawn of the railway age, and many attempts were made to meet the competition by using steam-powered road coaches. Goldsworthy Gurney, inspired by Trevithick's machine, which he had seen in Cornwall, built this steam carriage in 1829. It weighed two tons and carried eight passengers. It was said to have achieved 15 mph on its first section of the London-Bath run, but was attacked and damaged by a mob at Melksham, Wiltshire. Gurney continued to build his steam carriages, offering them for £1,000. In 1831 one of them provided a regular service between Cheltenham and Gloucester, doing the 18-mile round trip three times daily.

Published by Tho.ˢ Mᶜ Lean, 26 Haymarket, London.

PYALL Sculp.ᵗ

...eels to turn & direct the Carriage & another at his right hand connecting with the main Steam Pipe by which he regulates the motion of the Vehicle __ the ...cure principle, which is conveyed by Pipes to the Cylinders beneath & by its action on the hind wheels sets the Carriage in motion __ The Tank which ...ength & breadth __ the Chimneys are fixed on the top of the hind boot & as Coke is used for fuel, there will be no smoke while any hot or invihed air ...urney the Coach receives fresh supplies of fuel & water __ the full length of the Carriage is from 15 to 20 feet & its weight about 2 Tons _____ The rate of ...ies 6 inside & 12 outside Passengers, the front Boot contains the Luggage _____ ...n constructed by Mʳ Goldsworthy Gurney the Inventor & Patentee.

9

should tow cannon in the face of enemy resistance when horses might be killed. The military may have been impressed with the ingenuity of the inventor but not with his device's potential as a war machine. Cugnot's engine became merely an item mentioned in the army archives.

A somewhat similar three-wheeled engine was built by William Murdock, a Scotsman best known for his successful development of methods to produce gas from coal. Murdock's father had been a friend of Dr Roebuck, owner of the Carron ironworks and sponsor of James Watt's steam engine. As a result young Murdock got a job with the firm of Boulton and Watt and was sent to Cornwall as salesman and service engineer for the firm's pumping engines in the Cornish mines.

Murdock was an ebullient and ingenious man, who devoted his spare time to a host of experiments on any idea which aroused his interest. His steam locomotive was little more than a model standing only 3 feet high and mounted on three wheels, with a flue boiler and a single vertical cylinder working a beam connected to driving wheels at the rear. It made its inaugural and only run on a Sunday night in 1784.

Early inventions of this kind have their place in locomotive history but were isolated experiments yielding few practical results. The real pioneers of the science of steam locomotion were the men who had learned from experience that the use of a rigid track, with guide rails to act as a steering system, dramatically

lowered the tractive resistance of a wagon. In their daily work they knew how such tracks improved the capacity of horse- or manpower. Rails of various types had been in use in mine workings or at pitheads in Britain and Europe from the seventeenth century and probably earlier.

Richard Trevithick, the son of a Cornish mine manager, appreciated this from personal experience. He was a man who exulted in his strength, and often helped the tin miners push their wagons on the rails. He was also a brilliant engineer, building a mine engine himself when he was twenty-five, and in 1800 a double-acting 'strong steam' (high pressure) engine for the Cook's Kitchen mine. For years before this he was experimenting with model steam locomotives, and between 1801 and 1803 he built the first steam road carriage to carry passengers, and another which operated in London.

In 1803 he built and installed high pressure stationary engines at the Pen-y-darran ironworks near Merthyr Tydfil. The works had a 9-mile railway to carry iron ore, and with the approval of the owner, Samuel Homfray, Trevithick designed a steam locomotive to replace the horses, traditionally said to win a wager of 500 guineas that he could not make a mobile machine more powerful than a horse. Details of this engine are incomplete, but it is known that it weighed about five tons, the boiler was of the return flue type, the single cylinder was $8\frac{1}{4}$ by 54 inches, and it had a very large

opposite page **William Murdock's miniature steam locomotive, completed after experiments he began in 1784 at Redruth, Cornwall. Tradition has it that Murdock tried out his machine in the main street of the town late one Sunday evening. It careered past the church and terrified the parson, just leaving after evening service, who believed it to be a Satanic device.**

below **A model based on surviving details of** *Catch Me Who Can,* **built by Richard Trevithick in 1808. It hauled a wagon on a circular track near the present Euston station in London, offering a ride at 12 mph for a shilling. The small circumference of the track caused many derailments, and public interest soon declined. Thereafter Trevithick abandoned all interest in steam locomotives.**

flywheel to ensure smooth motion. It first ran on 13 February 1804, hauling twenty tons at an average speed of 4 mph.

Apart from proving that with high pressure steam a mobile steam engine could haul up to five or six times its own weight, Trevithick also demonstrated that adhesion between a smooth wheel and a smooth surface was good enough to provide traction. He developed the idea of wheels making contact with only a narrow surface in a locomotive he designed in 1805 for the Wylam wagon way at Newcastle. This engine, with a single horizontal cylinder driving a shaft connected to the driving wheels by toothed gears, is believed to be the first which had flanged wheels. The rails at Wylam were of wood. Whether the locomotive was tested on this unsuitable road, or whether it failed to operate efficiently, is unknown as it never went into routine service.

Despite the fact that Trevithick's Pen-y-darran locomotive successfully maintained track adhesion on a gradient of 1:18 the quandary remained that a sufficiently powerful locomotive was too heavy for the existing plateways and railways, while a lighter one produced insufficient power to compete economically with horses. A possible solution was provided by the rack railway. In 1811 John Blenkinsop, a Yorkshireman, patented a design for a toothed rail laid alongside the running rails, which was engaged by a cogged driving wheel on the locomotive. His claim was that by this method a locomotive no heavier than Trevithick's model could haul a load five times as great. Blenkinsop was associated with a Leeds engineer, Matthew Murray, whose firm, Fenton, Murray and Wood, was commissioned to build rack rail locomotives for the line

between Middleton colliery and Leeds, and subsequently for the Kenton and Coxlodge collieries on the Tyne.

The basic Trevithick design was used in these engines. The wood-lagged horizontal boiler was mounted on a heavy timber frame supported by four wheels, with the cog wheel for the rack rail between the left hand wheels. The double-acting vertical cylinders drove two shafts connected by gears to the rod carrying the cog wheel. The firebox was at the rear of the engine, but the boiler, strangely enough, had only a single flue, whereas Trevithick is believed to have adopted return flues from the outset of his experiments. For the purpose of operating on poorly laid track with very little grading the Blenkinsop engines proved their worth, and those used at Middleton remained in service from 1812 to 1835, undoubtedly the first locomotives which were a lasting commercial success for maker and customer.

The colliery owners of the North-East were implacable competitors in business, but at the same time formed a close-knit community of business men. They discussed the industry when they met at the annual hirings of labour held in the coal towns of Yorkshire and Tyneside. One proprietor, Christopher Blackett, was particularly interested in the haulage problem. His colliery at Wylam was five miles distant from the coal wharves at Lemington-on-Tyne. He was the purchaser of Trevithick's second locomotive, which had failed on the wooden rails. Blackett re-laid the line with cast iron plate rails in 1808, and ordered three of his employees, his blacksmith foreman Timothy Hackworth, a colliery overseer named William Hedley, and a handyman, Jonathan Foster, to carry out experiments and make him a locomotive. These men went about their job methodically, first building a manually-operated truck to check on factors of weight and adhesion, and the power needed to move various weights from rest on the rails. Hedley drew plans for a locomotive based on these findings, which was built for him in 1813 by Thomas Waters of Gateshead. It closely followed Trevithick's design, with a single cylinder and a large flywheel. The boiler was of cast iron and produced steam at a pressure of 50 pounds. The running wheels were powered through gears. Its capacity was roughly the equivalent of the hauling power of three horses and therefore an expensive substitute for animal haulage, though with fuel virtually free of cost, it was used for some months.

Meanwhile Hedley designed a more powerful engine, completed in 1814. The boiler was of wrought iron, there were two vertical cylinders fixed above the trailing wheels and working beams, with the driving rods connected to spur wheels geared to the driving wheels. Spent steam was carried by pipes to the chimney and vastly increased draught in the firebox immediately below the chimney. The problems arising during this quite revolutionary construction evidently created tensions, and Hedley and Hackworth parted company when the job was done. Apparently the dissension between the two men extended to the name of the locomotive, Hackworth calling it *Wylam Dilly* and Hedley describing it as *Puffing Billy*. Although the locomotive worked well, the old trouble of the permanent way arose. The plate rails rapidly broke under the engine's weight. To spread the load two additional pairs of wheels were added in 1815. These were given tractive power through gears from the original driving axles.

opposite page **Richard Trevithick, one of the pioneers of steam locomotion.**

below **In 1811 John Blenkinsop, a Yorkshire engineer, patented a rack rail engine, the cogged driving wheel engaging teeth cast on a rail on one side of the wagon rails. The engine had two double-acting cylinders and worked a payload five times as great as that of Trevithick's engines.**

bottom **The draughtsman's original drawing (side elevation) for Richard Trevithick's Newcastle locomotive completed in 1805 for the Wylam wagon way. This engine is believed to be the first to be built with flanged wheels. Another notable feature was a return flue boiler.**

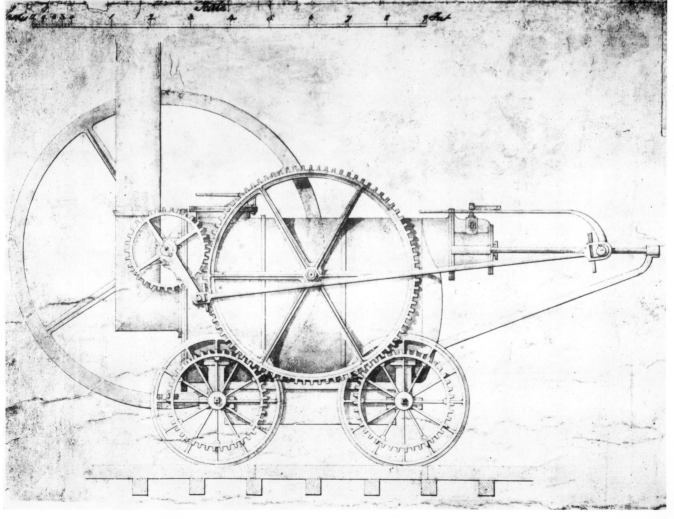

below *Wylam Dilly,* **photographed in 1862, when it was retired after nearly half a century of service at the Wylam colliery. Designed by William Hedley, and built by Jonathan Foster and Timothy Hackworth, this was basically the same as** *Puffing Billy,* **now in the Science Museum, London. It was completed about 1814.**

opposite, top **The original scale drawing of George Stephenson's Killingworth locomotive, built in 1815. The two cylinders had connecting rods taking power directly to the**

wheels, the axles of which were coupled by sprocket wheels and chains. The engine could haul 30 tons at 4 mph on a gentle gradient.

opposite, bottom **Model of** *Locomotion,* **the first engine built by Robert Stephenson and Co. It ran at the opening of the Stockton and Darlington Railway on 27 September, 1825, and could haul 50 tons at 5 mph on a level track. Weight on the rails was equalized by mounting one axle with its bearings inside a tube pivoted on the boiler.**

In 1830, when the track was re-laid with cast iron rails, the additional wheels were removed.

The Blenkinsop and Hedley-Hackworth locomotives were closely observed by George Stephenson, an engineer who had worked for years in various collieries on Tyneside. In 1811 he was working at the Killingworth colliery, and, encouraged by his employers, began experimental construction of locomotives. He subsequently claimed to have built a locomotive which first ran successfully in July 1812, but *Blücher,* named in honour of the Prussian Field Marshal and victor over Napoleon at the Battle of Leipzig, who was at the time visiting England, was the first to arouse interest. The locomotive followed the Blenkinsop design. The driving wheels ran on an iron rail designed by Stephenson, the type subsequently used for all railways. *Blücher* had a wrought iron boiler 8 feet long and about 3 feet in diameter. Two vertical cylinders of 8 by 24 inches worked the beams driving the wheels through a series of cogs, which caused noise and loss of power through friction. The Killingworth track had a steady uphill gradient in the direction used by loaded wagons, but *Blucher* proved capable of maintaining adhesion and a speed of 4 mph with a payload of thirty tons. This was

apparently its optimum performance and, like earlier engines, not economically competitive with horseflesh. Stephenson modified his design to use the exhausted steam by passing it through the chimney, thus improving fuel combustion and allegedly doubling the power of the locomotive.

He now began work on a new locomotive, abandoning the gearing in favour of direct connection of the piston rods to the driving wheels, the other two wheels being coupled to them by rods and cranked axles. Ball-and-socket joints between piston rods and axles helped to equalize the adhesion of all the wheels on the uneven track and to some extent eradicated the jarring and bumping which caused damage to the rails. The locomotive, completed in March 1815, had vertical cylinders at opposite ends of the boiler. The tender was in front, so that fuel was readily available for the front-end firebox. The coupled wheels were a great advance on the gearing system, but the cranked axles used for this purpose were weak and liable to crack, with the result that they were soon replaced with straight axles coupled by a chain rolling over sprocket wheels mounted at the centre of each axle. This coupling method was very effective until the chain stretched.

15

below A superb contemporary model of *Royal George,* an engine built by Timothy Hackworth in 1827 for the Stockton and Darlington Railway. He used parts of a locomotive built by Robert Wilson of Newcastle. A technical advance was direct drive to the wheels without chains or gearing.

opposite page Hetton colliery, near Durham, as an artist saw it about 1822. The Stephenson engines are not accurately portrayed and rails were apparently unnoticed by the artist. His object was to stress how steam power had completely taken over from horses.

1898·48

ROYAL·GEORGE Nº5

Eventually, the basic method of connecting rods fixed to the outside of the wheels was adopted.

Between 1816–22 George Stephenson built a series of locomotives of this type, and one is known to have had six coupled wheels. He was by now recognized as the leading authority on locomotive engineering. With the award of £1,000 he had received for his miner's safety lamp, and finance from two friends, Edward Pease and John Richardson, he started to build his own factory in Forth Street, Newcastle-on-Tyne, in August 1823.

The company was registered as Robert Stephenson and Co, a gift by 'old George' (though he was only forty-two) to his twenty-year-old son, the apple of his eye and graduate of the University of Edinburgh, having all the education that his father, who was illiterate until he was nineteen, had never enjoyed.

Apart from paternal affection and the desire to provide his son with every opportunity to exploit the family love of engineering, George Stephenson was moving into more promising fields than the construction of locomotives for colliery work. He envisaged long-distance railways to co-operate and compete with the canals in the transport of raw materials and merchandise, and with the stage coaches for passenger traffic. It is significant that in 1822, when he was appointed engineer in charge of the construction of the Stockton and Darlington Railway, he advised the directors to obtain authority to carry passengers as well as freight, and, of course, to use steam locomotives.

The first locomotive built at the Forth Street foundry was the 0-4-0 *Locomotion,* used to open the Stockton and Darlington Railway on 27 September 1825. It was basically of the Killingworth type, but with important

improvements. The valves of the vertical cylinders were driven by a loose eccentric. By mounting the axle bearings in a tube pivoted on the boiler, better equalization of wheel adhesion was ensured. The engine was heavier and more powerful, weighing about eight tons and capable of hauling fifty tons at 5 mph. This was a remarkably good performance considering the working steam pressure was restricted for reasons of safety to 25 pounds per square inch. Breakdowns were frequent, and the line was often worked by horses, but the troubles were clearly of a minor character, for *Locomotion* ran on the Stockton and Darlington line for twenty-five years before being relegated to duty as a colliery pumping engine. Three similar locomotives were built to meet the growing demand of traffic on the Stockton and Darlington line. They were named *Hope, Black Diamond,* and *Diligence.*

The aims of the management of the line were to provide a special kind of road on which anyone with a suitable vehicle could, on paying a toll, travel or transport his goods. If desired, means of haulage could be hired, but there was no compulsion to use this exclusively. A number of locomotives were built by enthusiasts to provide such facilities, and with their failure went into oblivion. One of these, the work of Robert Wilson of Newcastle, was fairly successful. This engine had four cylinders, two on each side, and all four directly driving the wheels without gears or levers. The wrought iron boiler was 13 feet long and 4 feet 4 inches in diameter. A U-shaped tube took the hot gases from the firebox to the far end of the boiler and then returned to escape through the chimney. This scheme greatly increased the effective heating area of the fire. The Wilson locomotive evidently had a disappointing performance, or at least had such potentialities

for improvement that the perfectionist and meticulous Timothy Hackworth, by this time employed by the Stockton and Darlington Railway, obtained permission to re-build it. He inverted the cylinders so that the connecting rods were shorter. He narrowed the flue exhaust pipe to increase draught. He made the bearings self-lubricating, with oil reservoirs above them. The safety valve was sprung instead of weighted. Hackworth used six wheels, 4 feet in diameter, and coupled them. Exhausted steam was used both to force-draught the fire and heat the feed water. Hackworth named his locomotive *Royal George.* The management of the railway kept careful records during *Royal George's* first year of service. It carried 22,442 tons of freight at a running cost of £466. The estimate for the equivalent work by horse-drawn transport was £1,000.

Hackworth built this engine without the direct aid of Robert Stephenson, who had left England for a tour of Central and South America in June 1824. He returned in November 1827 (incidentally bringing Richard Trevithick with him; he found the Cornishman penniless in Cartagena in Colombia, and lent him £50 to get home).

After his return, Robert conferred with his father on methods of reducing the size of their locomotives and making the mechanical side less complicated. They also tackled the problem presented by the fact that, if mobile steam power was to be used on the Liverpool and Manchester Railway, then nearing completion, the Government insisted that any engines used on it should consume their own smoke. In January 1828 Robert Stephenson, assisted by Henry Booth, who was the company treasurer and an amateur engineer of genius, began building a locomotive with a smokeless boiler. It was completed in July and put to work on the Bolton

Stephenson's *Northumbrian* by Nasmyth.

and Leigh Railway. This locomotive, *Lancashire Witch*, confirmed the inventiveness of the young Stephenson in his own right, for his father was too deeply involved in the construction of the Liverpool and Manchester Railway to do more than advise by letter. The boiler had two fireboxes and two flues, the forerunner of the multi-tubular boiler and Booth's valuable contribution to the design. The fires were fanned by bellows in order to ensure the efficient combustion of coke. The four coupled wheels were fitted with springs. Gearing, which cut off steam at half-stroke, improved economy in operation. The inclined cylinders drove crankpins on the leading wheels.

This engine did valuable work during the final stages of construction of the Liverpool and Manchester Railway, where its efficiency must have been apparent to James Walker and J. U. Rastrick, two engineers appointed by the railway's directors to report on the advantages and disadvantages of steam locomotives. In the winter of 1828–29 these two men toured many of the colliery railways using locomotives, but either through personal antipathy to the company's engineer, George Stephenson, or a cautious conservatism, they reported that they favoured stationary engines installed at one mile intervals. In fairness to them it must be said that the company hoped materially to augment the revenue from freight carrying by lucrative profits from passenger traffic, and the public attitude to the locomotive was a mixture of fear and derision–not without reason, considering the breakdowns and occasional explosions.

George Stephenson was prepared to risk his reputation on all-out support for locomotive working, and persuaded the directors to organize a contest with conditions demanding a better performance than any existing locomotive could meet, in order to prove once and for all that the future of railways lay with steam locomotive operation.

Those conditions were announced in April 1829. The deadline for entry was 1 October. In fewer than six months the nation's engineer's were challenged to design and complete the construction of a locomotive which consumed its own smoke, did not weigh more more than six tons, and did not exceed 12 feet in height to the top of the chimney. For reasons of safety boiler pressure was to be limited to 60 pounds, and the engine had to be capable of a continuous haul of a load equal to three times its own weight at an average speed of 10 mph. The price of the locomotive was not to exceed £550, including carriage to the railside. The winner would also receive £500.

The formidable conditions weeded out most of the would-be competitors. In the event only four steam locomotives were entered (the fifth was a contraption which somehow gained entry despite its ignoring most of the contest's conditions: it was a wagon operated by a horse on a treadmill).

That spring and summer the navvies on the railway saw little of George Stephenson. With their employees sworn to silence, George and his son worked day and night on a locomotive which, through the need for secrecy, could be tested only in theory and with steaming up for a run of a few yards. In mid-September the final touches were given: painting the frame and boiler in yellow and black, and the chimney in white. *Rocket* was ready for the Rainhill contest.

PIONEER LOCOMOTIVES

Of the estimated ten thousand people who streamed from Liverpool, and from as far away as Warrington and Manchester, to watch the locomotive contest at Rainhill, few expected to do anything but gloat over the failure of the weird and frightening machines to be put through their paces. *Perseverance,* built by Timothy Burstall, and *Cycloped,* the horse-operated machine, were quickly eliminated by failing to reach 10 mph. *Rocket,* with George Stephenson as driver, made its formal entry on 8 October. Its weight was $4\frac{1}{4}$ tons. The inclined cylinders of 8 by 17 inches drove the leading wheels, which were 4 feet $8\frac{1}{2}$ inches in diameter. The rear wheels supported the firebox. Despite its livery, it was not a handsome machine, and the high position of the cylinders, attached to the boiler by flimsy-looking brackets, gave an impression of inefficiency. What the observer could not see was the tubular construction within the boiler instead of the usual single flue or the double flue of *Lancashire Witch,* an advance which may have been adopted by the Stephensons after learning of data filed in France by Marc Seguin, who had patented the idea in February 1828. It set a precedent which was to endure until the last locomotives of the age of steam were built.

The trial course at Rainhill measured $1\frac{1}{2}$ miles, with extra distance at each end for starting and stopping, but the contest called for a total run of seventy miles – a rigorous test of the machines, which had continually to start, stop, reverse, and start again. *Rocket* suffered from vibration and jerkiness in motion, faults which were later alleviated by moving the cylinders to a lower position. But from the initial lap, *Rocket's* capacity could be in no doubt in the minds of the judges. It averaged 13·8 mph for the twenty double trips accepted as a complete trial, on one lap reaching 24 mph, with a load of $12\frac{3}{4}$ tons. On a demonstration run without wagons it averaged 29 mph from start to stop.

Novelty, built by John Braithwaite and John Ericsson, attractive in its livery of burnished copper and blue, had the appearance of a boiler, and little else, mounted on an ordinary wagon. All four wheels were 4 feet 2 inches in diameter. The firebox was sunk below the frame, with a bucket of fuel handy for the fireman in the centre of the wagon, and a water tank at the rear. The cylinders were 6 by 12 inches. Without water and fuel *Novelty* weighed only 3 tons. On a test run, with its light load to meet the conditions of hauling three times its own weight, *Novelty* reached 31 mph, but at the formal trials maximum speed was only 16·1 mph. On two separate days it failed to qualify by breaking down. Though the two engineers saw their hopes dashed they were later successful in building engines for the St Helens Railway. Subsequently, Braithwaite became engineer on the Eastern Counties Railway, and Ericsson found his real vocation as a marine engineer; he went to North America and built the famous *Monitor* which defeated the *Merrimac* during the Civil War.

After *Novelty's* withdrawal *Sans Pareil* was tested. The day allocated for the test, 13 October, provided another example of the bad luck Timothy Hackworth had suffered while building the locomotive. He had not been able to find workmen to carry out his ideas and despite all his theoretical checks the engine, when completed, proved to be too heavy to comply with the conditions. It weighed $4\frac{3}{4}$ tons and should therefore have been mounted on six wheels. However, the judges authorized its entry. The horizontal boiler had vertical cylinders of 7 by 18 inches, mounted on the sides and just above the rear end of the boiler. The driving wheels were 4 feet 6 inches in diameter. The tender was in front of the large and ugly chimney. For nine round trips the engine performed well, averaging close on 14 mph and on one lap reaching $17\frac{1}{2}$ mph with the stipulated load of 14·32 tons. When a cylinder fractured it was found to be only one sixteenth of an inch thick; it had been made for Hackworth by Stephenson, and there is a suggestion of ruthless determination to brook no competition in this instance of shoddy workmanship. Finally the feed pump broke, and *Sans Pareil* was out of the contest. Even before this misfortune the entry had little chance. Delays at the end of a lap were frequent, and consumption of water and fuel were heavy.

Thus *Rocket* was the unchallenged victor, and the Liverpool and Manchester Railway was committed to steam locomotive traction. The engine was immediately put to work hauling ballast and rails for construction of the final lengths of the line. It worked continuously until 1836, when it was bought by the Midgeholme colliery near Carlisle for £300 and used for some years hauling coal wagons.

As a result of the success of *Rocket,* the Stephensons received orders for seven similar locomotives. They incorporated improvements as construction went on. More tubes of smaller diameter were used in the boiler, and the cylinders were enlarged and moved close to a horizontal position. The best of these engines was *Northumbrian,* with the firebox as part of the boiler, used to haul the inaugural train on the public opening of the Liverpool and Manchester Railway on 15 September 1830. When *Rocket,* on the adjacent line, ran over William Huskisson, one of the MPs for Liverpool, the fatally injured man was placed in a truck previously used by a brass band due to play at the celebrations, and *Northumbrian* ran the fifteen miles to Eccles in twenty-five minutes, reaching 36 mph. It is appropriate that George Stephenson was the driver on what was probably the greatest sustained speed on a level course achieved by a man-made machine up to that time. *Northumbrian* later pulled the Duke of Wellington's carriage back to Liverpool, followed by a procession of trains hauled by *Rocket,* with Joseph Locke in charge, and followed by *North Star* and *Arrow.* Four other Rocket-type engines were on display that day: *Meteor, Phoenix, Dart,* and *Comet.*

The winner of the Rainhill locomotive trials:
Rocket, now in the Science Museum, London. The engine was
the combined work of Stephenson, father and son. George
produced the design and Robert, then only twenty-four,
supervised construction in co-operation with his works
manager, Michael Longridge.

below and opposite page *Pendennis Castle,* **a locomotive of the famous** *Castle* **class designed by C. B. Collett. The class was introduced in 1923 and built until 1950 in a series of improved versions.**

23

left **Robert Stephenson in his fifties, by then the first engineer-millionaire in history. After 1837, when he became chief engineer of the Birmingham Railway, his main interest was in building railways, and his speciality constructing bridges. The high-level bridge at Newcastle-on-Tyne and the tubular bridge across the Menai Straits were his triumphs.**

This reconstruction of *Novelty* **includes some of the original parts made by John Braithwaite and John Ericsson, the former already well known as the inventor of the donkey engine and the latter to gain fame as builder of the Monitor class turret battleship for the United States.** *Novelty* **was the favourite entry with the public at the Rainhill trials and was unlucky to lose because of mechanical defects. It was the first engine to run at a mile a minute, in 1829.**

The immediate and unexpected success of the Liverpool and Manchester Railway resulted in a demand for more powerful engines to handle the heavier traffic. Edward Bury, who had started his Liverpool engineering firm of Bury and Kennedy in 1829, was one of the leading contenders for this lucrative work. Bury was first and foremost a businessman, and left actual designing and supervision of construction to his partner, James Kennedy. Their early locomotive *Liverpool* was the first successful inside cylinder engine. The cylinders of 12 by 18 inches were placed under the smoke box, which was D-shaped. The coupled wheels were 6 feet in diameter. The inside bar frames of wrought iron were also the main frames, so that the wheels showed no extraneous fitments. The result was a sleek and functional machine which became one of a class, several of the name being built for both English and American customers.

Robert Stephenson learned something of the design drawings for *Liverpool* from his father, who was naturally involved in discussions about a contract issued by the Liverpool and Manchester Railway. Some of the ideas were adapted for Robert's 2-2-0 *Planet,* completed in October 1830. The inside cylinders of 11 by 16 inches were within the smokebox at the front, connected to a double-cranked rear axle with driving wheels 5 feet in diameter. The framing was of wood, but the main axle

25

A Stanier class *5* photographed in 1965 on a run from
Edinburgh to Manchester. This class of 4-6-0 locomotives
were known as *Black Fives* because of their black livery,
which indicated a mixed traffic engine. By 1951, 842 of these
versatile locomotives had been built.

5

Austria: ore empties from Hieflau nearing Eiseneiz behind a
class *86* 2-8-2 tank engine and a class *52* 2-10-0.

26

below **A drawing of the *Invicta*, built by the Stephensons for the Canterbury and Whitstable Railway, and embodying features of *Lancashire Witch*. It had to be small and light because of tunnels and a cheaply constructed track. The engine was brought by sea from Newcastle and made its first run on 3 May, 1830.**

bottom **An early lithograph of a first class passenger train on the Liverpool and Manchester Railway. The *Planet* class engines ran on the line from October, 1830 until the early 1840s.**

opposite page **The surviving remains of *Invicta* for comparison with the drawing of the complete locomotive. The boiler is 10 feet in length and the wheels are 4 feet in diameter.**

bearings were still outside the wheels. The weight was eight tons. *Planet* was a class name, and many of the type were built. For freight haulage all four wheels were coupled.

If the *Planet* locomotives had a defect it was the short wheelbase, causing pitching and hunting at the increased speeds which were becoming normal operational practice. As a result Stephenson designed his 2-2-2 *Patentee,* first operational in 1837. The 5-foot driving wheels of *Planet* were retained, but they had no flanges, the leading and trailing wheels keeping the engine on the rails. The cylinder stroke was increased to 18 inches and the weight went up to $11\frac{3}{4}$ tons. The *Patentee* type, with improvements over the years, opened up railways all over the world, and engines basically of the same design were being built up to the last decade of the nineteenth century.

The belief that mechanized railways were only profitable for comparatively short hauls of heavy and bulky freight died slowly. As a consequence, people in the little industrialized South-East of England remained unmoved at the news from the industrial North. However, there was an exception. For a long time a need had existed for a cheap means of transporting import and export merchandise between the towns of Kent and the Thames estuary without ships sailing as far as London. Plans for a canal were shelved in 1824 in favour of a railway, originally to link the Thames with the Sussex coast at Shoreham, but finally restricted to a route between Canterbury and Whitstable. The Stephensons built *Invicta* for the railway, embodying much of the design used for *Lancashire Witch*. The inclined cylinders of $10\frac{1}{2}$ by 18 inches were placed over the front wheels and drove the 4-foot rear wheels. The 10-foot long boiler had a single flue. The inaugural run took place on 3 May, 1830. Meantime, on the site of

TRAVELLING on the LIVERPOOL and MANCHESTER RAILWAY.

the first successful railway at Darlington, Timothy Hackworth was devoting his skill to the construction of powerful locomotives for freight work. His powerful 0-6-0s, with either vertical or inclined cylinders, which became known as the *Majestic* class, were among the best engines of their day. Two of his locomotives represented important advances. *Wilberforce*, completed in 1832, had a large steam dome from which pipes ran to the cylinders, which were 14¾ by 16 inches. To produce the head of steam needed for such a large capacity, Hackworth designed a main flue which carried the hot gases along a conduit tapering to 2 feet at the combustion chamber, from which the gases returned through rows of copper tubes to the smokebox. The final version of these Hackworth designs was *Derwent* built at Darlington by Alfred Kitching and Co in 1839. This 0-6-0 locomotive had inclined cylinders of 14½ by 24 inches driving wheels 4 feet in diameter.

below *Joem,* **an 0-6-0 tank engine, storms the last hundred yards into Haworth station.**

opposite, top **Steam and sky – a goods engine silhouetted against the sunrise at an iron quarry in Northants.**

opposite, bottom **The Mount Washington cog railway.**

EARLY AMERICAN ENGINES

It was probably inevitable that Britain, as a victorious nation in the Napoleonic Wars and as the country in the forefront of the industrial revolution, should be the birthplace of the steam locomotive. She had the stimulus and the resources of skilled men and materials. But the concept of harnessing steam to create mobility was a natural development of a machine age the impact of which was worldwide, and which in particular inspired the young and resourceful nation in North America, where the pioneer spirit was as strong for the creation of industry as for opening new territories.

The Napoleonic Wars and the War of 1812 between Britain and America did not seriously inhibit the exchange of information and the advance of international science. Faraday and Davy visited most of the universities of Europe in the midst of the turmoil of the Napoleonic Wars. American and English businessmen and engineers did not consider the War of 1812, and its aftermath, any hindrance to corresponding about the machines hauling coal at English collieries. To many Americans these engines appeared to confirm their own theories about the potentialities of steam power as a means of transport. American scientists had long devoted thought to the idea, though hampered by the lack of skilled craftsmen and a tradition of engineering.

If he had been born twenty years later, the American Oliver Evans might well have ranked with the Stephensons as a successful early inventor of the steam locomotive. Evans realized that a much higher pressure of steam than that achieved in stationary steam engines was essential to make a mobile machine a practical proposition. Improved metallurgy made it possible for him to construct a boiler producing 60 pounds per square inch by 1815, which then earned him, at the age of sixty, the title of 'father of high pressure steam'.

Evans was a visionary, and his imagination marred the practical side of his work. He tested a self-moving steam engine on Christmas Eve 1801, and had a geared engine running on cast-iron plate rails by 1803. His most curious device he named the *Oructor Amphibolis,* designed to run on land and propel itself in water. It trundled from the factory yard in Philadelphia as far as the Delaware river, where it sank. Subsequently Evans devoted himself to propaganda, writing in 1812 about a future when passengers would 'breakfast in Baltimore, dine in Philadelphia, and sup in New York'.

The realization of that dream was many years distant. A more practical approach was taken by Colonel John Stevens, a wealthy resident of Hoboken, New Jersey. He had been impressed in 1787 when watching the experiments of John Fitch with a steam-propelled boat on the Delaware. In 1804 Stevens designed a screw-driven steam boat, which operated successfully on the Hudson river. However, his real interest lay on the land, and through political influence he obtained a charter to build a railroad to be operated by steam

locomotives from New Brunswick to Trenton. This was in 1815 and is regarded as the first charter of its kind in the United States. The move was, of course, no more than gesture to the future, but Evans' ideas stimulated ceaseless experiment. In 1825, this grand old man of seventy-five proudly demonstrated a model locomotive running on a half-mile track in the grounds of his house. A notable, and at the time novel, feature was a multi-tubular boiler. Power was transmitted through a ratchet and cog wheel. Though his own inventions were never commercially successful, before he died in 1838 Evans had seen many of his ideas applied to locomotives running in a dozen areas of the United States.

The forward-looking culture of a young nation made Americans more ready to accept the new invention than many financiers in England, and hopeful schemes to exploit it were adopted in principle before the resources existed for manufacture. Consequently, engines were ordered from England. The first locomotive to run commercially in the New World was unloaded at New York in July 1829. It had been purchased for $3,000 from the Stourbridge firm of Foster Rastrick by the engineer of the horse-operated track at Honesdale, Pennsylvania, belonging to the Delaware and Hudson Canal Co. *Stourbridge Lion* worked well but was too heavy for the track, which crossed a number of flimsy trestle bridges, and its use was soon abandoned.

The inaugural run of the *Stourbridge Lion* on 8 August 1829 was watched by a young engineer, Peter

Cooper, employed by the Baltimore and Ohio Railroad. In its brief life the railroad had considered, and sometimes tried, various methods of traction, including horse-operated windlasses, stationary steam engines, a horse-operated treadmill car, and even a car equipped with sails. Cooper, working in the company's sheds at Mount Clare, completed his engine by August 1830. His aim had been to minimize weight as compared with English models. The result was ugly, and the Cooper locomotive was promptly dubbed 'a tea kettle on wheels'. The upright boiler was in the centre of an ordinary wagon, the cylinders driving one pair of wheels through a gear and ratchet. The official name was *Tom Thumb*. Despite its appearance, the engine was technically sound. In its inaugural run it hauled a car carrying the directors and their friends along the fourteen miles of the railroad in $1\frac{1}{4}$ hours. The company next offered contracts for American-built locomotives – two to be bought for $4,000 each and two for $3,500 each. Maximum weight was to be $3\frac{1}{2}$ tons and they were to be capable of hauling fifteen tons at 15 mph. The announcement was made on 4 January 1831, and the engine was to be ready for trial by 1 June.

Only one man accepted the challenge: Phineas Davis, a New York watchmaker. His locomotive was as peculiar in appearance as *Tom Thumb,* but beautifully engineered. The upright boiler, mounted in the centre of a small truck, had vertical pistons, and power was transmitted to all four wheels through cranks. It passed

opposite page *Stourbridge Lion,* an English locomotive built by Foster, Rastrick and Co, was the first steam locomotive to run on a commercial track in the United States. It first ran on 9 August, 1829, along a track built for the Delaware and Hudson Canal Co between a wharf at Honesdale, and the mines at Carbondale. This picture was painted for the centenary of the engine's debut.

below Peter Cooper's *Tom Thumb,* built in 1830. It was a scientific model rather than a working locomotive, designed to convince businessmen of the potential of the steam locomotive.

its trials and was used on a regular passenger service between Baltimore and Elicott's Mills, covering the distance in under an hour. Davis was rewarded with the $4,000 prize – and the post of Master Mechanic to the Baltimore and Ohio. His next locomotive was *Atlantic.*

Meantime, in New York State, the forerunner of the New York Central Railroad was born with the construction of the 15-mile line between the Mohawk and Hudson rivers. The inspiration for this project came from George Featherstonehaugh, a wealthy immigrant from England, who was farming in Schenectady County. He returned to his homeland with Peter Fleming, an engineer employed on building the track, to study English methods. Both Featherstonehaugh and Fleming spent two years, and most of their personal resources, on constructing the line over difficult terrain. They were succeeded by John B. Jervis, who was an enthusiast for steam locomotives in preference to horses and stationary cable engines, both of which

the directors favoured. Jervis commissioned the West Point Foundry to build a locomotive. The result was the historic *De Witt Clinton,* named after a popular Governor of New York, which first ran on 9 August 1831. Its weight was a little over three tons, the overall length 11½ feet and its four wheels were 4 feet 6 inches in diameter. The inclined cylinders, fixed to the rear section of the horizontal boiler, were 5½ by 16 inches, and drove the front wheels, which were linked to the rear wheels by connecting rods.

De Witt Clinton was worked very hard, reportedly attaining 30 mph, and was worn out within two years. Unfortunately it was scrapped soon afterwards. By then an English locomotive had been purchased, named *Robert Fulton,* but on account of its origin known as *John Bull.* In 1838 it was almost entirely rebuilt, only the English boiler being retained.

This *John Bull* locomotive was not the official one of that name. Stephenson's *John Bull* arrived in New

35

York in November, 1831, for operation on the Camden and Amboy Railroad, running from the Delaware river to Raritan Bay, a distance of sixty-one miles. A routine product of the Stephenson works, *John Bull* was fitted with the characteristic long American funnel to minimize the danger of setting fire to roadside crops and property, and with a cowcatcher. It once again proved the reliability of the English locomotive, robust because because of its comparatively heavy weight, and reliable through the technical skill of Stephenson's labour force. *John Bull,* after years of normal operation, was exhibited at the Philadelphia Centennial in 1876 and at the Chicago Exposition of 1883. It was then placed in the National Museum at Washington until 1893, when under its own steam it hauled a train to the Chicago World's Fair, gave some 50,000 passengers rides that summer, and then steamed back to Washington.

The reputation of English locomotives created a flourishing trade to supply traction for the new American railroads. A particularly attractive engine was *Stephenson,* with green-painted wooden lagging on the boiler, and embellished with black bands. This locomotive was running on a 26-mile road between Boston and Lowell in 1835. Rather unwillingly English engineers were adapting locomotive design for special American requirements. Apart from the widespread use of wood as a fuel, necessitating modification of the firebox, the curves on American tracks made some kind of guide wheel essential. John B. Jervis, builder of the Mohawk and Hudson Railroad, is credited with the invention of the bogie, which he called a swivelling truck, ahead of the driving wheels. The term bogie was supposed to be a derisive term given by Stephenson's employees, though it was in widespread use among Northumberland miners to describe their pit wagons hauled by women in the shafts.

Robert Stephenson supplied a 4-2-0 sandwich-frame locomotive for the Saratoga and Schenectady Railroad in 1833, *Davy Crockett.* The order, placed by John B. Jervis, the chief engineer, stipulated that a 4-wheel truck should 'connect the frame of the forward wheels with the crosspiece by a king pin at the centre only, thus enabling these wheels to turn freely on curves'. *Davy Crockett* was an outstanding success from the day of its maiden run on 2 July 1833, the public regarding the service as a pleasure ride to the extent that freight was largely ignored in favour of the more profitable passenger traffic. Its average speed was scheduled for 17 mph, and in good weather 3,500 passengers a week enjoyed their first experience of mechanized railroad travel.

American engineers had to attempt to provide light machines to run on railroads built on restricted budgets and originally constructed for slow horse-drawn wagons. A typical instance was the Lexington and Ohio Railroad. The track consisted of pieces of limestone on which iron rails only half an inch thick were laid. A section of the line was opened with a horse-drawn car in August 1831, while a steam locomotive was being built. This was to the design of Thomas H. Barlow, credited with the invention of the modern planetarium, in partnership with Joseph Bruen. It was not ready until March 1833. Only a few details of this locomotive, and an improved version completed in January 1834, survive. It was said to be 'not more than three or four feet high, wheels, boiler and all'. It had twin perpendicular cylinders, and a bizarre feature was the rope

below *De Witt Clinton* was built by the West Point Foundry, New York, in 1831, and made its first commercial run on 9 August of that year on the 14-mile line of the Mohawk and Hudson Railroad between Albany and Schenectady. It averaged 18½ mph. The engine was developed from the upright-boilered *Best Friend of Charleston,* built by the same firm in the previous year.

bottom Sixty-two years after her first run *De Witt Clinton* was in working fettle once more–at the Chicago World's Fair in 1893. The three coaches were replicas.

tiller to guide a pilot wheel. Apparently these locomotives, named *Nottaway* and *Logan,* were really road tractors running on the limestone blocks with the cars they hauled having flanged wheels running on the rails. As might be expected, the diminutive size and wheel contact with a rough running surface resulted in serious lack of tractive power. Passengers were regularly ordered out to push engine and car up any slope, and a profitable sideline by the engineman was the hiring of a horse for 25 cents for the alarming downhill stretch to Frankfurt, when the locomotive restricted speed with difficulty.

One of the most successful of the early American-built locomotives was the *Best Friend of Charleston,* ordered for the 6-mile track of the Charleston and Hamburg Railroad in South Carolina. Details of this engine are vague but it was apparently a lighter version of English locomotives. It was built at the West Point Foundry and shipped to Charleston in December 1830. On 15 January 1831 it made its inaugural run, with an exciting burst of 25 mph. Thereafter it worked freight and passenger cars regularly until tampering with the safety valve resulted in the boiler exploding. The engine was later repaired and appropriately re-named *Phoenix*. A sister locomotive, *West Point,* operated on the line which was being extended until it reached Hamburg.

below *America*, **built by Robert Stephenson for the Delaware and Hudson line, combined features of both** *Locomotion* **and** *Rocket*. **Because the track was unsuitable it was soon used as a stationary engine.**

centre *Davy Crockett*, **a 4-2-0 engine for the Saratoga and Schenectady Railroad, was one of the most successful of the early locomotives in the United States, due largely to the 4-wheel truck at the front making for reliable running on curves. It first ran on 2 July, 1833.**

bottom **Ugly but useful: the** *Oregon Pony* **built for Union Pacific in 1862. Small workaday engines of this type were built in their hundreds for work on permanent way maintenance, in marshalling yards, and frequently for short-run services on struggling narrow-gauge lines.**

opposite, top *Lafayette* **built by the Norris brothers of Philadelphia for the Baltimore and Ohio Railroad in 1837, marks the emergence of a distinct American style—a leading bogie and long wheelbase. Engines of this type were sold to Britain for the Birmingham and Gloucester Railway in 1840.**

opposite, bottom *York,* **built by Phineas Davis in 1831, won a $4,000 prize in a contest stipulating a maximum weight of 3½ tons. It ran between Baltimore and Elicott's Mills on the railroad subsequently named Baltimore and Ohio.**

By then the railroad had a third locomotive, *Baldwin,* the work of the man who founded what was to become one of the world's largest locomotive engineering works. Matthias Baldwin was a manufacturing jeweller in Philadelphia; at the request of the local museum he built a miniature locomotive to run on a circular track, which operated successfully on 25 April 1831. This model impressed the management of the horse-operated Philadelphia, Germantown and Norristown Railroad, and Baldwin was commissioned to build a steam locomotive. His first was *Old Ironsides.* This was based on the design of Stephenson's *Planet,* and was an extremely handsome machine. The rear driving wheels were 54 inches in diameter, powered by 9½ by 18 inch horizontal cylinders mounted on the outside of the D-shaped smokebox. The iron wheels were 45 inches in diameter. The boiler, 7 feet in length, contained 72 copper tubes. The total weight was five tons. Baldwin had great difficulty in finding skilled labour, carrying out much of the work personally. One of his problems was sealing steam joints, where he had to use canvas coated with red lead; this soon rotted and had to be constantly renewed. *Old Ironsides* was, however, a great success from the day of her inaugural run on 23 November 1832. Baldwin was a perfectionist, and saw more faults in his locomotive than his customers did. He said he would build no more locomotives. However, the continuing success of *Old Ironsides* brought orders, not only from South Carolina, but from the Philadelphia and Columbia line. Baldwin's engine for this company was *Lancaster.*

In the Deep South, the railroad fever had struck in Louisiana as early as 1825. Reports on colliery locomotives in England had suggested the advantages of a railroad connecting the waterfront of New Orleans with Lake Pontchartrain as a faster method of transport than the existing canal. An enterprising resident named Lambert, who had patented a design for a steam locomotive, was praised in the press as 'a benefactor

Scale one inch to the foot. —

Original drawing of the West Point the second Locomotive Engine
First Train on the United States made by the South Carolina Rail Road

opposite page **A plan of the American locomotive,** *West Point.*

below *Mississippi,* **operating on the Natchez and Hamburg Railroad, along the basin of the Mississippi river, was typical of the all-purpose locomotives of the small systems which sprang up in the Southern States before the Civil War. This engine was a wood burner; the canopy is a later addition.**

of mankind when at last he brings his improvement to perfection'. Whether the locomotive was ever built or tested, let alone improved and perfected, is unknown. However, planning of the railroad began in March 1830. Rails and a locomotive were to be bought in England, but the order for the engine was cancelled, presumably for financial reasons. The line was opened in April 1831 with horse-drawn cars. The first steam locomotive was built by John Shields of Cincinnati. No details of it survive. It was, in any event, a failure and was relegated to work as a power lathe in the railroad workshops. The standard Stephenson export locomotive was thereupon purchased and was at work by September 1832.

Another historic American railroad was the Northern Cross, partly financed by the legislature of the new State of Illinois, of which Abraham Lincoln was a member. It was planned to run from Quincy on the Mississippi, through Jacksonville and Springfield, to the Indiana State line. A locomotive was ordered from England, but records show it was 'lost in transit', presumably through shipwreck. A contract was hastily given to the engineering firm of Rogers, Grosvenor and Ketchum of Patterson, New Jersey. *Rogers* made its

inaugural run on a 12-mile section of line completed west of Jacksonville, covering it in two hours.

News of American progress in engine building made a big impression in Europe, and resulted in orders for locomotives to be shipped across the Atlantic for the railways under construction in the German States. Hitherto the Stephenson *Patentee* had been virtually the standard locomotive to make the inaugural run on a European track, as on the Nuremburg-Fürth line in 1835 and the first section of the Netherlands Railway from Haarlem to Amsterdam in 1839.

But German engineers were anxious to enter this lucrative business, and US locomotives were bought for trial and examination. The Baltimore firms of Gillingham and Winans supplied a vertical cylinder 2-2-2 for the Leipzig-Dresden line in 1836, and features of this engine were combined with those of the *Patentee* to create a German-style machine. By 1841 Maffei in Munich and Borsig of Berlin had produced their first locomotives: Maffei's *Munchner* and the Borsig *Beuth,* forerunners of an output which was to put Germany alongside Britain and the United States as the leading locomotive builders.

ADVANCE
OF THE IRON HORSE

In Britain the railway fever broke out with deceptive slowness. It reached its height, spawning dozens of get-rich-quick schemes having little result beyond fortunes for a few and losses for hordes of investors, well after the United States had experienced economic depression in 1838–40 and was marking time on future developments.

Most of the minor enterprises in England were in time absorbed by the larger companies, and it is in the origins of the trunk lines that the story of locomotive development continues. The first was the Grand Junction Railway, authorized by Parliament in 1833 to build a line from Birmingham to link up with the Liverpool and Manchester line. Joseph Locke, a former pupil and employee of George Stephenson, was in charge of the major section of the work. Close on the heels of the Grand Junction project came the London and Birmingham, built by Robert Stephenson under an Act also passed in 1833. The Grand Junction was opened in 1837 and the final stage of the London and Birmingham was completed in 1838. The locomotive department of the latter was under the control of Edward Bury, whose firm was by then re-named Bury, Curtis and Kennedy. He set up his base at the hamlet of Wolverton, roughly midway between London and Birmingham. The capital was thus linked with the two most important industrial areas of England.

The bar-frame type of locomotive, first seen in Bury's *Liverpool,* became the normal type on the London-Birmingham route: 2-2-0s for passenger trains and 0-4-0s for freight. These engines were light and inexpensive, and therefore attractive to the managements of companies which were faced with financial problems and had tracks built as cheaply as possible. The Bury engines were, in any event, assured of use on the London and Birmingham line, their maker being in the delightful position, as locomotive superintendent of the line and partner in the firm given the contracts, to build the engines for it.

In the West Country, citizens of the wealthy seaport of Bristol had considered projects to link the Avon with the Thames by some means of land or water route as early as 1824. In 1832 a group of businessmen formed the Bristol Railway Committee, and in March 1833 engaged Isambard Kingdom Brunel, designer of the Clifton suspension bridge, as chief engineer. He was twenty-seven years old. It was not until August 1835 that the Great Western Railway received government authority to start building. Approval of Brunel's gauge of seven feet and a quarter-inch was obtained two months later. One small section, between West Drayton, Middlesex, and Langley, Bucks, was completed in December 1838. The deputy engineer to Brunel, Daniel Gooch, who was twenty-one, had by then assembled *Vulcan,* made by Tayleur's Foundry and delivered in sections by canal. Gooch had also purchased a locomotive, *Premier,* from Mather Dixon and Co. These

An artist's romantic impression of the inaugural run on the Canterbury and Whitstable Railway on 3 May 1830, painted for the edification of the directors. In reality, the ceremony was not quite so happy, for the engine had difficulty in managing the gentle gradient from Whitstable. Stationary engines were later installed to pull trains over some of the hilly sections.

two engines made test runs during the early days of 1838, with disappointing results, the major problem being constant derailment—a fault possibly to be ascribed to the permanent way rather than to the engines themselves. Brunel had stipulated a minimum cruising speed of 30 mph at a time when engineers regarded it as a maximum. The wide body and long axles for running on a gauge of seven feet and a quarter-inch presented difficulties in making a heavy and unwieldy engine both stable and rapid.

The official opening of the Great Western Railway took place on 31 May 1838, with a train from Paddington to Maidenhead. It was hauled by the most reliable engine out of the eighteen the company had by that time purchased. *North Star* was one of four supplied by Robert Stephenson. The others were *Morning Star, Evening Star,* and *Dog Star.* All had been under construction when the Brunel contract was offered and were intended for the Pontchartrain railroad at New Orleans, but the order had been cancelled. The United States gauge was 5 feet 6 inches, and Stephenson simply widened the frames and lengthened the axles to adapt his engines for the GWR. Thus they did not have any of the dubious refinements and changes other engineers were trying out for the wide gauge. All the *Star* engines were virtually identical, with cylinders of 16 by 16 inches and a boiler heating surface of 711 square feet. *North Star* possibly had the edge as regards speed, with driving wheels of 7-foot diameter compared with wheels of 6 feet 6 inches on *Morning Star* and, it is believed, on the others.

After the driver and fireman had learned how to nurse *North Star,* and some improvements had been made to the track, this engine was soon averaging 38 mph for the 25-mile journey as a scheduled service. The locomotive was in continual operation until 1854, when it was rebuilt and worked for a further sixteen years before being retired to the Swindon works.

The complete GWR route from London to Bristol was opened on 30 June 1841, with a junction to the partially completed Bristol and Exeter Railway, so that the inaugural train from Paddington could run through to Bridgwater, covering the London-Bristol stage of 118 miles in four hours and the entire run of 152 miles in 5½ hours.

The Great Western's rival, the London and Southampton Railway, was originally an adaptation of a scheme, devised under the pressure of war, to evade naval attack by the French in the Channel by conveying Southampton imports by canal to London. The possibilities of a rail connection were considered during the winter of 1830–31 after the Rainhill trials. The usual problems of getting finance and overcoming Parliamentary resistance delayed the approving Act till July 1834. Bury supplied a light locomotive, *Lark,* in 1835 for hauling ballast and excavated material. Joseph Locke took over the engineering work as soon as he had completed the Grand Junction Railway, and the London-Woking section began operation in May 1838, with Joseph Woods, the locomotive superintendent, organizing the motive power, which he purchased from Sharp, Roberts, the Rennies, and Rothwell. All the engines were based on Stephenson's *Patentee* design.

The complete line was open to traffic in May 1840, and soon afterwards John Gooch, brother of the Great Western's Daniel Gooch, was appointed to run the locomotive works. The first engine he designed, *Eagle,*

below **Isambard Kingdom Brunel, chief architect and engineer of the Great Western Railway from 1833 to 1846. In 1835, aged twenty-nine, he wrote in his diary: 'The railway is now in progress. I am the engineer to the finest work in England. A handsome salary of £2,000 a year, on excellent terms with the directors, and all going smoothly'.**

opposite, top *North Star,* **built by Robert Stephenson and Co for the New Orleans Railroad, was shipped back to England owing to financial disputes. It was then adapted for the 7-foot gauge of the GWR and was an outstanding success, working until 1870. The photo shows a replica built for the railway centenary celebrations of 1925.**

opposite, bottom **The success of** *North Star* **influenced Daniel Gooch in his design of 2-2-0 express locomotives which became the standard on the GWR after 1840. More than sixty of them were built in two years. They were about three tons heavier than the Stephenson engine.**

Lion was built in 1838 for the Liverpool and Manchester Railway by Todd, Kitson and Laird. After twenty-one years' service this 0-4-2 was bought by the Mersey Docks and Harbour Board, and was eventually converted into a stationary pumping engine. It was restored in time to participate in the series of centenary celebrations of the 1920s and '30s. In the photo, Lion is hauling replicas of the six coaches used in its early years.

was built in the new works at Nine Elms in south London in 1843. By then the name of the railway had been changed to London and South Western, and was largely responsible for the emergence of Southampton as a major port for passenger ships.

In this formative period of the railway age, a young engineer whose name was to become a household word was learning his trade. Alexander Allan was a junior employee of Robert Stephenson during the construction of the Patentee. He then moved to the foundry of George Forrester and Co in Liverpool, which had contracts to build locomotives for the Liverpool and Manchester Railway and for the line opened from Dublin to Kingstown (now Dun Laoghaire) in 1834. These handsome engines had double frames with horizontal cylinders at the front, mounted on the outside, and driving the rear wheels. The first delivered to Ireland was named Hibernia. The wide space between the cylinders and the long cranks produced a swaying motion with the result that the drivers named them 'Boxers'. This emulation of a pugilist taking evasive action was partially rectified by adding a trailing axle so that the Forrester engines are the forerunners of the six-wheeled outside cylinder locomotive.

The 0-4-2s built in 1838 by George and John Rennie, who had been appointed engineers in the early days of the Liverpool and Manchester project, followed the Forrester cylinder pattern, and owed much to Patentee, though the Rennies would not have admitted it, being bitter rivals of the Stephensons on both commercial and personal grounds. The Rennie locomotives were the first to have double frames, with the driving wheel axles in the inner frames and the trailing wheels held by axle boxes on the outer frames. They were built for the London-Croydon Railway, a short section of which was opened in June 1839.

Another small railway which stimulated design and production of the 2-2-2 outside cylinder engine was the Arbroath and Forfar Railway; fiercely Scottish with a gauge of its own devising – 5 feet 6 inches – it opened for traffic in January 1839. The engines were built by Stirling and Co of Dundee, and embodied a number of innovations. The cylinders were steeply inclined, 13 by 18 inches with valves on the top. The 5-foot driving wheels were held by the inside frames only. To improve steadiness in running, the cylinders were subsequently lowered to a horizontal position. The drivers were increased to 5 feet 5 inches. These locomotives became almost a standard type for the early Scottish railways.

Although engineering firms building locomotives were springing up in every large town where skilled men were available, the Stephensons were still virtually unassailable as the prosperous pioneers. Apart from the flourishing trade with the United States, the Patentee type brought steam locomotion to many countries in Europe. The first locomotive seen in Germany was Stephenson's Der Adler (The Eagle), supplied to the

below **Borsig of Berlin analysed the designs of both British and American locomotives and combined the best features of both. This engine, completed in 1845, is reminiscent of Stephenson's** *Patentee*, **by then busy on European lines.**

opposite, top *Earl of Berkeley,* **a rebuilt Dean 4-2-2, preserved on the Bluebell Railway. This class was designed to be converted from broad to standard gauge and specialized in long non-stop runs.**

opposite, bottom, **A winter train on the Keighley and Worth preserved railway approaching Haworth behind** *Peckett No 1999.*

railway built between Nuremburg and Fürth. The project had been the idea of a Bavarian mining engineer, Josef Ritter von Bader, who had become friendly with Trevithick and Blenkinsop when studying colliery practice in England, and a colleague of his, Johannes Scharrer.

The newly-formed German Customs Union encouraged railway construction in order to turn the political alliance into an industrial reality, and locomotives were bought from many sources in order to study their design and performance. The firm of Gillingham and Winans of Baltimore, Maryland, supplied a 2-2-2 inside cylinder engine, *Columbus,* for the Leipzig-Dresden line in Saxony, and in 1839 William Norris of Philadelphia built a cumbersome 0-4-0 vertical boiler engine, with intricate gearing between the vertical cylinders and the driving wheels, for the Berlin-Potsdam railway in Prussia. A much more attractive locomotive from Norris was *Austria,* a 4-2-0 outside cylinder engine lavishly embellished with brass and

bronze, which first ran in 1838 on a section of the horse-operated railway between Linz and Budweis (now České Budějovice). *Austria* shared the work with a Stephenson *Patentee,* purchased a year earlier. By 1840 German engineers were producing their own designs and creating an identifiable European type. Maffei of Munich built *Number One,* a 4-2-0 with the front bogies well forward of the outside cylinders, making for very steady running. Borsig of Berlin followed the same design but increased the size, adding a pair of trailing wheels. These two firms, subsequently eclipsed in size by Krupp of Essen, were to put Germany alongside Britain and the United States as the world's leading engine builders. In the early years they experienced problems in engaging designers and skilled craftsmen, which was one reason why Germany was prepared to go to the expense of buying engines and bringing them across the Atlantic, unassembled in crates. All early German engines combined the best features of both the Stephenson *Patentee* and the United States leading bogie type.

DEVELOPMENT OF POWER

Routine maintenance and repair work on the popular *Patentee* engines revealed that the smokebox was often damaged by intense heat, evidence of wasted energy. To make better use of the hot gases, Stephenson patented his long boiler design in 1841. Previously boilers had rarely exceeded 9 feet in length. In the new model it was $11\frac{1}{4}$ feet. Although the diameter was slightly reduced the heating surface was increased to 800 square feet, as compared with an average of 650 square feet in Stephenson's earlier engines. In order to keep down costs he used wrought iron (and subsequently steel) instead of brass or copper for the tubes. The size of turntables on most railways limited the wheel base to 12 feet. To meet this need Stephenson placed all the axles between the firebox and smokebox. Other economies were achieved by simplifying construction, using a single-plate frame instead of sandwich frames, and by placing the valves between the cylinders in one steam chest.

The first 2-2-2 long-boiler locomotives went into service in 1841 on the York and North Midland Railway and the Northern and Eastern Railway. In the early models the cylinders of 14 by 20 inches were the inside type. In 1844 2-2-2s withoutside cylinders were built. Driving wheels were 5 feet 6 inches in diameter, which gave a potential of high speeds, but the 2-2-2s were liable to yaw seriously at more than 30 mph, and despite Stephenson's anxiety to maintain a low centre of gravity by restricting the height of the boiler, the wheel base was really too short for such an engine. However, as the long-boiler engines were reliable in service and economical in operation, large numbers were bought for railways in Britain and overseas.

Rather more satisfactory was the 2-4-0 freight and mixed traffic version, which first appeared in 1842, but the large rear driving wheels restricted the size of the firebox, and though the long boiler made good use of the fuel 2-4-0s could not be worked as fully as the general design suggested.

Another version of the 2-4-0 appeared in 1845. This had outside cylinders placed further back to relieve the weight on the front wheels and the first pair of driving wheels. However, the major success of the Stephenson long-boiler locomotive was in its 0-6-0 freight version. For hauling heavy loads, with frequent stops and periods of shunting, the engine was without equal, and versions of it were in production at the Newcastle works for more than twenty years, the type becoming the standard for freight locomotives all over Europe as well as in Britain. The type known as the *1001* class, built after 1860 for the Stockton and Darlington Railway, represented the ultimate design. The diameter of the original cylinders had been increased from 14 to 17 inches and steam pressure rose from about 80 pounds to 130 pounds. These engines were still in operation in Britain after the First World War, and there are probably still some in eastern Europe.

Derailments were frequent in the early years of railways, alarming a public still wary of the new form of travel. Ingenious and often impractical ideas emerged, evading the only real solution: construction of a solid, well-graded track, which was costly. Prosser's patented guide wheels, set at an angle as leading and trailing wheels on engine and carriages, were tried on the 8-mile line between Guildford and Woking in Surrey. The happy scene of a train descending a steep gradient, and engines negotiating tremendous curves is, of course, artistic licence.

below **A preserved** *No 103* **4-6-0, one of D. Jones' 'Jones' Goods' mixed traffic engines. Introduced on the Highland Railway in 1894, they were the forerunners of the modern 4-6-0 mixed traffic engines.**

In 1843 the Grand Junction's Crewe works were opened. Francis Trevithick, son of the Cornish inventor, was put in charge of locomotive construction, assisted by the youthful Alexander Allan. The first engine made at Crewe was a 2-2-2 with outside cylinders. *Columbine* was a workmanlike, neat engine and weighed only 18 tons – a feature appealing to the railway management, which favoured small, light locomotives, easy to build and inexpensive to run. At a time when money was being squandered in a frantic battle to attract investors and gain publicity, this conservative policy was unusual, but it built a lasting reputation for the Trevithick-Allan engines. Between 1845 and 1858 the Crewe works turned out 378 of them, including a 2-4-0 freight version.

The *Columbine* type also became the standard on the railways in France. While Allan had been manager at the Edge Hill works of the Grand Junction, prior to the opening of Crewe, his superior was William Buddicom. The general design of *Columbine* had been discussed by the two men, and when Buddicom took the post of superintendent of the Paris and Rouen Railway, he persuaded an old friend and ex-pupil of Robert Stephenson, William Allcard, to come with him and set up a locomotive foundry at Rouen. The business flourished by turning out the Crewe type of engines. While steam traction lasted on French railways a 2-4-0 was described by railwaymen in that country as *un Buddicom*.

The Grand Junction was not amalgamated with the London and Birmingham to become the LNWR until 1846. The two railways had followed very different policies as regards locomotive design, with the newly-appointed James McConnell in the south determined

53

below **Alexander Allan's** *Columbine*, **built in 1845 for the Grand Junction Railway. This 2-2-2 became known as the Crewe type and large numbers were built up to 1858, becoming a standardized basic design for engines in both Britain and Europe. They were the first locomotives successfully to work the tough gradients of Shap in Westmorland.**

opposite, top **Daniel Gooch's** *Firefly* **class for the GWR. Gooch was appointed superintendent of the line when he was only twenty-one. His design exploited the advantages of the broad gauge, with a heavy engine having greater boiler capacity and a higher steam pressure than previously used. The Gooch link motion economized on fuel and made better use of steam.**

opposite, centre *Little England*, **built by George England in London and shown at the Great Exhibition of 1851. It was designed for light railways of the kind then being built in many parts of the world. The makers claimed that it was capable of hauling a train carrying 10 passengers at 45 mph with a consumption of only 7 pounds of coke per mile, an economical performance of great appeal to struggling companies.**

opposite, bottom **An engraving of the GWR locomotive** *Iron Duke.*

to build powerful engines capable of speeds unheard of on the route to the North-West. McConnell was young, critical of the 'old guard', and patriotically determined to see that England maintained her place in the lead. This determination had been roused while he was employed by the Birmingham and Gloucester Railway, which included a formidable gradient of 1:37 in the Lickey Hills. There was then no English locomotive manufacturer prepared to guarantee reliable working on such an incline, with the result that in 1840 Norris of Philadelphia was asked to supply the first American engines to work on an English line. They were 4-2-0s with inclined cylinders of $10\frac{1}{2}$ by 18 inches, the driving wheels being only 4 feet in diameter. The Norris engines were slow but sure; the first engines weighed $9\frac{1}{2}$ tons and later engines weighed 13 tons. With the object of restoring English honour, McConnell had completed by 1845 the most powerful engine in existence at that time in Britain: a saddle tank locomotive for banking work on the Lickey gradient. *Great Britain* weighed thirty tons, and by what amounted to sheer force effortlessly propelled every load up that formidable gradient.

McConnell thus came to his impressive new job at

Wolverton with an almost fanatical faith in the still only partially tapped power of steam. His first design, in 1849, was for a 2-2-2 express locomotive with outside cylinders. It had outside frames and bearings, and proved too wide for the platforms on the line, which had to be cut back after the engine's wheel bearings had fouled some of the stonework. This earned the engines the name of 'Mac's Mangles', and if they earned McConnell some derision from the public he was, within a couple of years, to gain their admiration with some of the most revolutionary express engines of the mid-Victorian age.

Prior to the developments at Wolverton the resourceful Daniel Gooch of the GWR in collaboration with his chief designer, T. R. Crampton, was supporting Brunel's contention that the broad gauge was the most suitable for heavy rolling stock and fast working. The outcome was *Firefly,* a larger version of *North Star,* embodying the overall design of Stephenson's *Patentee,* completed in 1840. *Firefly,* forerunner of a famous class, had 7-foot driving wheels, the 6-foot version being named *Fury.* Cylinder diameters were 15 inches and 14 inches respectively. Swindon was not at the time ready for engine manufacture and these GWR locomotives were built under contract by many of the well-known foundries of the day. It says much for the meticulous work of Gooch and Crampton that they could specify

details of materials and methods which resulted in a standardized engine, whatever its origin. At a weight of only 24 tons the *Firefly* class proved superbly steady at high speeds. Though precise recordings of speed were not then feasible, there is ample evidence that the GWR engines easily attained 75 mph running light, and there is the historic event on the opening day of the line from London to Exeter, when a *Firefly* covered the out-and-return journey of 387½ miles at an average running speed of 40 mph.

This was the formidable proof of good performance that the GWR took to the Royal Commission, appointed in 1845 to decide on a uniform gauge for the whole country. Brunel, confident that train performance would decide the issue in his favour, then suggested a series of trials.

The broad gauge tests were held between Paddington and Didcot. Daniel Gooch used *Ixion,* a 7-foot single driver, and *Hercules,* a six-coupled freight engine. *Ixion* hauled carriages weighing sixty tons and averaged 50 mph, start-to-stop, over a series of runs.

The standard gauge interests, which in effect were all the other large railways and their financiers, selected a straight and level stretch between York and Darlington. Combing the country for the best engines, the rivals of Brunel chose two Stephenson long boilers for the express tests and a six-coupled freight engine

Great Central Railway 0-4-0 locomotive *No 506, Butler Henderson,* **built in 1920.**

(also named *Hercules*) for the load trials. One of the express locomotives left the rails on the second day and was damaged; the other, a 4-2-0 named *Great A,* went through its paces, but gave a disappointing performance. Despite the far better speeds of the broad gauge locomotives the Commission came out in favour of the 4 feet 8½ inches gauge. From 1846 further construction using other gauges became illegal, with the exception of some minor and specialized lines.

Almost as a gesture of defiance Gooch then designed the first of his 8-foot single drivers. *Great Western* was one of the first engines built at the new Swindon works. From idea to completion the project took thirteen weeks. Its cylinders were 18 by 24 inches. The boiler gave a heating surface of 1,733 square feet with steam at 100 pounds pressure. Gooch gave *Great Western* a couple of months to settle down. Then in June 1846 he told its crew to show what they could do. With a train weighing 100 tons *Great Western* averaged 59·3 mph from Paddington to Swindon; it ran on to Exeter to average 51·1 mph for the entire run.

Great Western was followed by *Iron Duke* in 1847. This was the first of the standard GWR express engines, which operated until the broad gauge was abolished. The first engine weighed 35½ tons, a great weight for the time, and this was subsequently increased, the last ones made weighing 41½ tons. Steam pressure was increased from 100 pounds to 120 pounds.

Many of the engines in the *Iron Duke* class have become legendary. In 1848 *Great Britain* made a scientifically checked run from Paddington to Didcot, start-to-stop, at 67 mph. *Lord of the Isles* was shown as an example of British locomotive design at the Great Exhibition of 1851. The so-called Crimea group aroused patriotic fervour by being named after battles in the Crimea War–*Alma, Balaclava, Crimea, Eupatoria, Inkerman,* and *Sebastopol.*

The ambitious Crampton, who may have felt his talents were in danger of being repressed in the severely practical atmosphere of Gooch's design office, left the GWR to set up as an independent engineer and contractor. He visualized remunerative contracts if he could offer an engine able to compete with his previous employer's *Iron Duke* class. He designed a boiler which combined a low centre of gravity and a large heating surface with driving wheels of 7-foot diameter placed behind the firebox. Thus the greater part of the weight was on the forward section, with one pair of wheels under the smokebox and a further pair below the centre point of the boiler. Crampton received an order from the Namur and Liège Railway for two of these engines, and he was enterprising enough to persuade the LNWR to try out the first one completed, *Namur,* on their own lines. The trials were impressive, the engine running light at 75 mph and hauling a typical express at up to 50 mph with plenty of reserve power. In the brief period of the tests the effect of a locomotive weighing close to thirty tons, and pressing hard down at the fore-end when running fast, on the soft iron rails of the southern section of the LNWR was not noticed. It was, however, to be a major objection later. But at the outset the Crampton engine, a really new and unusual design, brought Crampton rich rewards. *Namur* and her sister engine impressed European managements, and orders came from lines all over France and Germany, close on 300 being supplied up to 1864. As late as 1889, a Crampton on the Paris-Lyon-Mediterranean Railway reached 89·5 mph, hauling a passenger express weighing 157 tons. The French Cramptons were made by the Paris firm of Derosne et Cail.

For the LNWR Crampton designed a slightly larger version of *Namur*. It was built by Bury, Curtis and Kennedy. The forward part was carried on six wheels and the drivers were 8 feet in diameter. Two, called *Liverpool* and *London,* were completed in 1848.

Crampton's patent for placing the boiler below the driving axle was utilized by Francis Trevithick in his design for *Cornwall,* a locomotive of bizarre appearance,

with driving wheels of 8½ feet. In fact the top of the barrel was slightly above the level of the axle, and the flue tubes were just below it. Thus there was a groove across the middle of the boiler and two domes to collect steam from two sections. Another peculiar feature was that the axle of the rear running wheels ran through an iron tube housed in the firebox itself. As originally designed *Cornwall* was a 2-2-2, but it was modified to a 4-2-2 after trials. Its heating surface was 1,000 square feet, and the engine was designed to work at a pressure of 120 pounds per square inch. Despite the complication

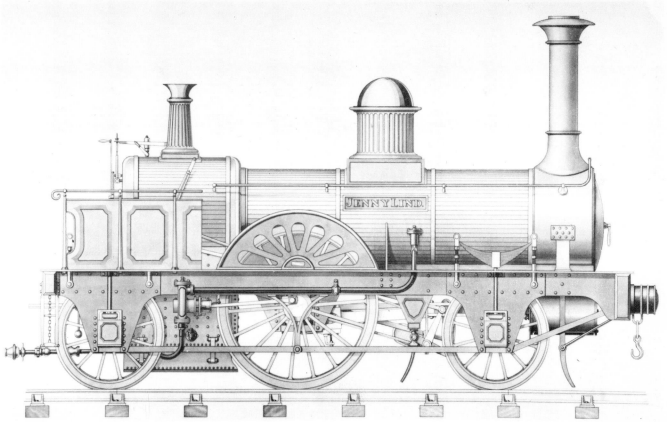

of this remarkable design *Cornwall* caught the public fancy, probably on account of its huge driving wheels, which suggested power and speed. The engine was eventually rebuilt, again as a 2-2-2, with a conventional boiler above the driving axle. From 1858 to 1902 it worked expresses in the North-West, and thereafter it pulled an engineer's saloon inspection coach until 1922, a useful working life of seventy-five years, though with considerable rebuilding at intervals.

The preoccupation with the need to place the boiler as low as possible for reasons of safety, which was originated by Stephenson and reached its extreme in Trevithick's *Cornwall,* was discontinued by John Gray, and later by David Joy. Gray had been in charge of locomotives on the Hull and Selby Railway before he moved to the London, Brighton, and South Coast Railway. While in charge of the Yorkshire line he designed some inside cylinder, mixed-frame 0-6-0 engines in which the boiler was unconventionally high so as to clear the axles of the 5½-foot wheels. Gray also adopted a mixed frame for the 2-2-2 express locomotives he had designed between 1840–44. On his appointment to the Brighton line he continued to order the 2-2-2 design, most of the orders going to the E. B. Wilson foundry at Leeds where since 1844 David Joy – only nineteen at the time – had been in charge of the drawing office. In 1847 Gray asked Joy to visit him to discuss a design for some new express engines. On Joy's return to Leeds, and in the course of a single weekend at his home, he completed the general

outline of his design for a 2-2-2, with inside frames stopped at the firebox and outside frames for the leading and trailing wheels. With a boiler of 10½ feet, using 2-inch diameter tubes, he obtained a heating surface of 800 square feet, and he made the best use of it by specifying a working pressure of 120 pounds. The first of these sweet-running engines was aptly named *Jenny Lind,* in honour of the 'Swedish nightingale' who in the year of the engine's debut, 1847, first appeared on the London stage.

Locomotives of new appearance naturally created widespread interest among engineers and the public. Equally important were the developments made in improving the mechanical efficiency whatever the general design. Gray patented his horse-leg valve gear, which varied the steam cut-off in the cylinders. It was fitted to locomotives on the Hull and Selby Railway after 1840.

Belgium was unique among small countries in encouraging railway engineers. The original motive was to achieve economic independence after separating from the Netherlands in 1830. In 1834 the Belgian government approved a plan for a 154-mile railway from Antwerp to Aachen and Cologne. Three Stephenson engines, *Elephant, Stephenson,* and *Arrow,* opened the first section from Brussels to Malines in 1835, their success earning George Stephenson a Belgian knighthood. British designs were always a feature of Belgian railways, the engines either imported or built at Liège.

opposite page **LNER 4-6-2** *No 4472, Flying Scotsman,* **hauling a special train through Bramley to Carlisle and Newcastle.**

below **A preserved Great Western tank engine. She was built in 1936 at a cost of £2,247, and bought in 1964 by the Great Western Society for £750.**

bottom **An ex-Southern Region 0-6-0 tank engine entering Ingrow with a southbound train on the Worth Valley Railway.**

ERA OF EXPERIMENT

J. E. McConnell's 2-2-2 design of 1849, derisively dubbed his 'mangle', was followed by a class which can be ranked as one of the best on the southern section of the LNWR system. McConnell's ambition was to build a locomotive capable of providing a two-hour express service between London and Birmingham. The large boiler gave a total heating surface of 1,449 square feet producing steam at 150 pounds. The inside cylinders of 16 by 22 inches were fixed to inside frames and there were no outside bearings – a feature which gained these engines, on their debut in 1851, the nickname of 'Bloomer' because of the absence of 'skirt'.

The first of these 2-2-2s appeared in 1851. They were the mainstay of the express services but had not the capacity to give a two-hour run from London to Birmingham. Accordingly McConnell designed a larger version, intended to take advantage of the legal relaxation on smokeless fuel restrictions. Driving wheels were $7\frac{1}{2}$ feet and the cylinders were enlarged to 18 by 24 inches.

McConnell had a kindred spirit, and a doughty competitor, in Archibald Sturrock, a Scotsman who had learned his trade in the Stirling foundry at Dundee and had then worked under Daniel Gooch at Swindon. In 1850 he was appointed locomotive and carriage superintendent of the Great Northern Railway, which that year had run its first train from London to Peterborough and was on the brink of achieving amalgamations and running rights to Edinburgh. Sturrock, ambitious to make the line better than the west coast route to Scotland, and familiar with the high speeds of the GWR broad gauge engines, aimed at running expresses on the 393 miles from London to Edinburgh in eight hours.

In 1853 he designed a 4-2-2 (known by its number, *215*). It had $7\frac{1}{2}$-foot driving wheels and inside cylinders of 17 by 24 inches. The firebox closely followed the broad gauge dimensions so that Sturrock was in practice almost doubling the fire area, as compared with most engines on the standard gauge lines. As a result he was able to obtain steam pressure of up to 150 pounds, a fact which on the advice of his previous employer he kept to himself, in case it aroused alarm among drivers and the public. The associated companies of the Great Northern system were not, however, impressed with the attractions of advertising an eight-hour service between the English and Scottish capitals, and *215* was relegated to mixed working.

Sturrock thereupon designed his famous *Large Hawthorns,* a 2-2-2 double-framed locomotive built for him by R. and W. Hawthorn. They weighed 33 tons and worked heavy main line traffic, twelve of them being built from 1855–6.

Sturrock was always a 'power man', sometimes with theories which did not work out in practice. In 1863 he brought out his auxiliary engine in the tender of 0-6-0 freight engines, based on an idea which had been tried out in France twenty years before. His instructions to

An artist's impression of a Gooch *Bellmouth* on the London
Metropolitan Underground, over which the GWR had
running rights. The line between Bishop's Road and
Farringdon Street was opened in January, 1863, with broad
gauge for the GWR section. Gooch's engines were the first
with condensing tanks to get rid of exhausted steam, and
twenty-two were built. They were not an unqualified success.

opposite, top **Locomotive *No 1* of the Achenseebahn at the terminus on Lake Achensee, Austria.**

opposite, bottom **Inside the cab of** *King George V.*

below **J. E. McConnell's *Bloomer* locomotives were designed for express work on the southern division of the LNWR. Forty of the standard type were built after 1851, and immediately**

impressed the travelling public with their powerful lines and large boilers.

bottom **With the aim of providing a 2-hour service between London and Birmingham three extra-large *Bloomers* were introduced in 1861. There were also smaller versions used on fast, stopping trains. All had an imposing livery of scarlet.**

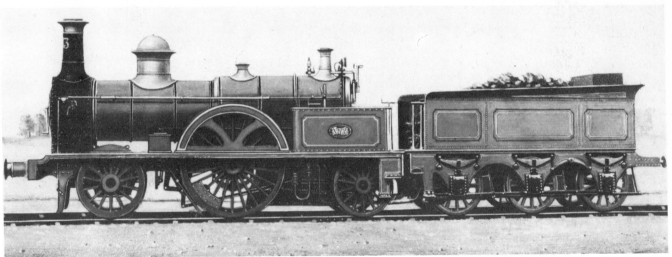

drivers to build up steam pressure meant that there was plenty to spare when a locomotive started up or was running slowly. He also wanted to obtain more adhesion. He coupled the wheels of a six-wheeled tender and built in a pair of cylinders of 12 by 17 inches, which were fed through flexible pipes. Nearly fifty were built between 1864–66, but they were costly in fuel, the pipes leaked, and the crews complained of the complicated extra work.

The 1850s saw rapid development of the tank engine. Many were, of course, light locomotives for work on branch lines, usually with single drivers. More impressive were the broad gauge tank engines introduced in 1853 on the Bristol and Exeter Railway. Designed by J. Pearson and built by Rothwell and Co of Bolton, these were the first English engines to make real use of the bogie, so long adopted in the United States. These 4-2-4 locomotives had inside plate frames and cylinders of $16\frac{1}{2}$ by 24 inches. The wheels on the bogies were 4 feet

in diameter and the 9-foot flangeless driving wheels, with no splashers to hide them, were as high as the top of the boiler. Required for high speed work on a hilly route of a maximum of fifty-six miles, the Pearson tankers had adaptability for shunting and easy turnround, plus the power required for express work. Speeds of 80 mph were regularly attained.

Another innovation of the period was the general adoption of 0-6-0 locomotives for heavy freight trains. Notable among them were those introduced to the Midland Railway in 1852. They were designed by Matthew Kirtley, who had been appointed locomotive superintendent of the Midland on its formation in 1844. Kirtley was one of those self-educated men who became expert designers and builders of railway engines. At the age of thirteen he had gone to work on the Stockton and Darlington Railway, and when old enough he became fireman on the London and Birmingham, shovelling coke on the first train to run when the line was opened.

65

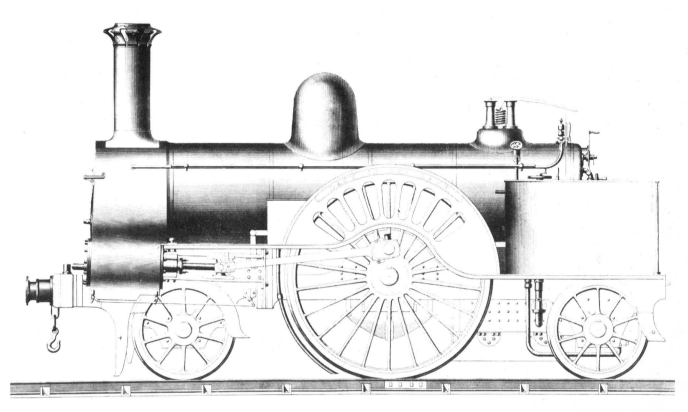

As head of the Derby works he directed the mechanical side of a line which was to become one of the wealthiest in Britain.

Ideas for burning coal efficiently, instead of coke, had been tried out with varying success for some years. They all had the defect of being complicated. McConnell at Wolverton extended the firebox and divided it into two with a water-filled partition. Joseph Beattie of the LSWR devised a double firebox with a coke fire in one section to burn the surplus gases from the coal, and in another version a firebox of two compartments with a glowing fire forward and the new fuel burned in the rear section. Kirtley and his colleague Charles Markham proved that all these complications were unnecessary. By building a brick arch below the boiler's tube plate and a deflector plate in the firedoor, bituminous coal could be burned to yield its energy without waste and with a minimum of smoke.

The pollution problem was a considerable factor with the opening of the world's first underground railway, London's Metropolitan line between Paddington and Farringdon Street, on 10 January 1863. Stephenson built a single driver with hot firebricks to maintain steam during the twenty-minute run. It was called *Fowler's Ghost* and was unsuccessful. The more practical aid of Daniel Gooch came to the rescue with a design for the first condensing tank locomotives to go into service. They were 2-4-0s, with outside cylinders

and 6-foot coupled wheels. A more efficient system of curbing fumes was devised by Beyer, Peacock and Co in the 4-4-0s subsequently ordered by the Metropolitan. The condensing system was based on bypassing exhaust steam from the blast pipe into another pipe which entered the top of the tank. These locomotives were ideal for the start-stop operation involved. The leading wheels were at first on a Bissell truck, but after 1871 Beyers used a sliding bogie. The engines ran on the Metropolitan underground section until electrification in 1905, and then went on working on the suburban extension and on the provincial and European railways to which they were sold. A few continued to give trouble-free service after half a million miles, and the last of them was not withdrawn from the Metropolitan line until shortly before the Second World War.

Developments and changes in railway operation, such as the underground system, stimulated the new generation of engineers. At Crewe John Ramsbottom took over from Trevithick in 1857. He was a fine craftsman and technician and, perhaps as important in the history of British locomotives, a great administrator. He studied the existing 0-6-0 freight engines and standardized the basic design so that parts were interchangeable, not only within a particular class, but as much as possible from one class to another. His first standard engine in the *DX* class appeared a year after he joined the LNWR. In the following sixteen years 943

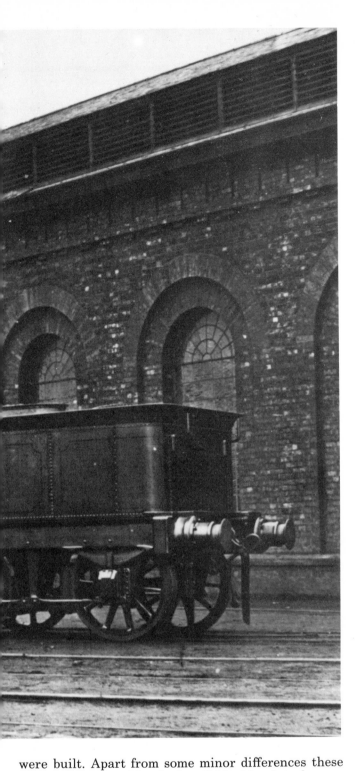

left *Lady of the Lake No 531.* **The very large tender is noteworthy on this pretty little locomotive. The Ladies needed plenty of fuel and water so as to make long runs non-stop. They were the first in the world to pick up water while in motion, and a sister of the engine shown,** *No 229 Watt,* **earned a record with a non-stop run of 104 miles between Holyhead and Crewe in 1862.**

below **The first passenger train at Auckland, New Zealand leaving the dockside for Onehunga on Christmas Eve, 1873.** *Ada* **was an 0-6-0, coal-burning locomotive.**

enough. Crewe could make a locomotive as much as 50 to 75 per cent cheaper than other workshops.

With the lucrative freight traffic adequately catered for, Ramsbottom began the design of light, inexpensive passenger express engines, though 'express' was almost a euphemism when compared with the ambitions for speed on other lines. The LNWR regarded an overall speed of 40 mph as adequate for long distance work – a speed defined as the maximum by Queen Victoria when she travelled by train, a stipulation causing some exasperation to the GWR when they ran the royal train between Paddington and Windsor.

Ramsbottom's 2-2-2 engines were deceptively small. They weighed 27 tons, and the overall appearance was dwarfed by their driving wheels of 7 feet $7\frac{1}{2}$ inches. The horizontal outside cylinders measured 15 by 24 inches and the axles had inside bearings only. They were the first English engines to be fitted with an injector to supply water to the boiler, a device invented in France by Henri Giffard in 1859.

The Ramsbottom 2-2-2 was originally known as the *Problem* class. Their reputation quickly earned them a more attractive name: *Lady of the Lake.* Sixty were built between 1859–65, and for nearly half a century they went back and forth over the northern section of the LNWR. All were named in a haphazard style. They included *Napoleon, Star, Saracen, Marmion* (the engine which took part in the 'races' to Scotland in 1888), and *Mersey.*

The American Civil War placed the British government in a delicate situation, and the crisis worsened when the USS *San Jacinto* stopped the British vessel *Trent* and took off some Confederate passengers. The reply by Washington to Whitehall's note of protest was regarded as deciding whether Britain would actively participate in maritime action to protect British shipping in American waters, and possibly enter the war. The reply arrived by the mail packet at Holyhead on January 7, where Ramsbottom had a special train waiting. The engine was a *Problem* class, *Watt.* Thanks to the water trough pick-up system Ramsbottom had invented and installed on the northern section of the LNWR in 1860 the engine was able to run non-stop the $130\frac{1}{2}$ miles to Stafford at an average of $54\frac{1}{2}$ mph.

The *Problem* class was followed by Ramsbottom's 2-4-0s. They were simple, workmanlike engines with outside plate frames and inside cylinders of $16\frac{1}{2}$ by 22 inches. The early version, first operating in 1863, and usually known as the *Samson* class, was intended for branch line and stopping services. This type proved so economical and reliable that they were followed by a larger one, the *Newton* class, in 1866.

were built. Apart from some minor differences these locomotives were identical: solid inside plate frames, inside cylinders of 17 by 24 inches and wheels of 5 feet 2 inches. The heating surface, at 1,102 square feet, produced steam at a pressure of 120 pounds. They also included an important innovation, Ramsbottom's screw reversing gear.

Engines which could be seen by the dozen on the LNWR every day, identifiable one from another only by a number, obviously deprived the Ramsbottom freight engines of the glamour which enthusiasts had come to look for, with their individual designs and prominently displayed nameplates. From a business viewpoint Ramsbottom pioneered a practice which has since been emulated by every manufacturer of machinery. Critics of his day might have deplored this rationalization, but railway managements were happy

RAILS WORLDWIDE

By the middle of the nineteenth century American locomotive design had moved markedly away from the British prototypes which new railroads had imported in the early years as an almost automatic gesture to instil confidence in the stockholders. Developments in Britain had been almost entirely directed towards requirements in the domestic market, where the demand was for fast operation with light loads, the trains running on solidly built and carefully graded tracks. These newer engines, mechanically reliable and expertly constructed, were not really suitable for the robust conditions of America, where profitable pay loads were more important than speed.

The doyen of American locomotive builders, Matthias Baldwin, used his sixteen years of experience to design the first heavy United States engine, *Governor Paine,* delivered in 1848 to the Vermont Central Railroad. It had the conventional 2-2-0 wheel arrangement, the driving wheels were 6½ feet in diameter, and the large boiler produced enough steam to enable the engine to start from rest and complete a mile in forty-three seconds when running light. With a load of freight it trundled along almost inexorably at a steady 15 mph.

This was a more successful American innovation than the 1844 experiment of the Baltimore and Ohio which put into service an 0-8-0 with a complicated arrangement of gears connecting two sets of coupling rods. Its weight and uneven motion resulted in the track being pounded, even at slow speeds, and it was called 'Mud Digger' during its brief life.

The obvious solution was to obtain tractive power with coupled wheels, and to distribute weight and enhance steadiness with a leading bogie. Thus the wholly characteristic American general purpose locomotive came into being, namely the outside cylinder 4-4-0. This type had been first built by Henry Campbell for the Philadelphia, Germantown and Norristown Railroad in 1837, and belatedly recognized as an ideal design, so that the type was being produced in quantity by the 1850s by every private firm and railroad with a building works. Very few of the 31,000 miles of track in the United States on the eve of the Civil War were without this workmanlike engine, with its characteristic balloon or lantern chimney; most engines still burned wood, though a few were experimenting with bituminous coal and anthracite.

When civil war broke out in 1861 the Confederate States had about a quarter of the nation's total railroad mileage and proportionately far fewer locomotives. The big locomotive manufactuers were in the North and East. Where the Southern States boasted locomotive works they were really assembly shops. The main exception was the Tredegar Ironworks of Richmond, Virginia, where Joseph Anderson turned out forty locomotives after 1850. They were the usual 4-4-0s, with 5½-foot drivers and outside cylinders. Most of them ran on the Virginia Central Railroad, and were greatly

The New World's most memorable railroad photo: the ceremony after the last spike had been hammered home at Promontory Point, Utah, on 10 May, 1869, completing the transcontinental route. Central Pacific's *Jupiter,* on the left, moved slowly forward until the crews on the front could shake hands with those on Union Pacific's *No 119.* The chief engineers of each railroad, Montague of CP and Dodge of UP, are shaking hands in the centre of the picture.

below **Locomotive building in the nineteenth century was the most lucrative branch of engineering. Salesmen ranged the world with beautifully made models of their wares, while catalogues provided illustrations and technical data. This page from a list issued by Baldwin of Philadelphia shows typical US types of engine. The top picture shows what was the most successful type – the 4-4-0 for moderately fast work with heavy loads on poor tracks. The 0-8-0 (lower left) was for working heavy freight on severe gradients. The 4-6-0 was the prestige model for passenger expresses hauling coaches far heavier than anything then known in Britain. All three** models were offered in a variety of sizes, according to customer's requirements and financial resources.

bottom **A Currier and Ives lithograph, showing an Erie Railroad express near Jersey City in 1870.**

opposite page **Another Currier and Ives lithograph, showing two *Lightning Express* trains steaming away from a junction in New York State in 1863. Of interest are the passenger coaches with bogies. Such coaches were not introduced in Britain until 1874.**

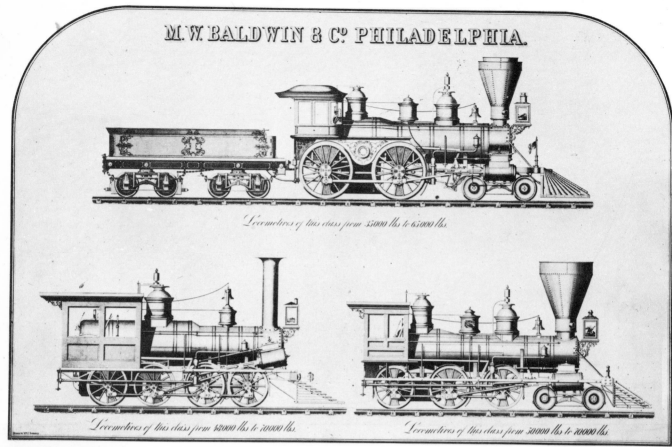

M.W. BALDWIN & Cᵒ PHILADELPHIA.

admired for their ornate appearance. The fierce individuality of the mass of small companies in the South encouraged distinctive decorations on their locomotives. Typical was *Thomas Furse,* built in 1860 for the Central Railroad of Georgia. It carried panels on its sides in which were displayed oil paintings depicting the Goddess of Liberty, the Savannah Exchange, and two portraits of Furse, a director of the company.

Unlike the Northern railroad companies, which usually confined engine descriptions to numbers, those in the Southern States followed the British practice of naming their locomotives. The Virginia and Tennessee line used names of local beauty spots. The North Carolina adopted the names of Greek gods. All flattered notabilities and investors–with named engines. After war broke out this sometimes caused embarrassment. *United States* and *General Scott* had to be hurriedly changed to *Confederate States* and *General Beauregard.*

The Civil War was the first major conflict in which the steam locomotive became a sinew of war. Rail communication played an important, possibly decisive role, with all the advantages on the Union side. Those reliable 4-4-0s moved men and materials on a scale never previously attempted. In 1863 thirty trains worked day and night to move 25,000 troops over 1,200 miles from the Potomac to the upper reaches of the Tennessee river. Throughout the war, General Sherman's sabotage groups reduced the Confederate lines to a shambles, destroying their overworked and patched-up locomotives and rolling stock.

The war proved that the railroad could bind a great nation as no other method could. It also encouraged the concept of a coast-to-coast line. The Bill for the Pacific Railroad was signed by Abraham Lincoln on 1 July 1862. Work began at Omaha on the Union Pacific road in December 1863, and the first lengths of rail were laid in July 1865. By then two locomotives, *General McPherson* and *General Sherman,* were available for hauling men and construction materials. The latter engine hauled the train carrying the General in person for a formal inspection trip in November some thirty miles west of the Missouri. By September 1866 the line reached the 100th meridian, 243 miles west of Omaha. The inaugural train was hauled by the 4-4-0 *Idaho,* with Vice President Durant riding in the car which had borne the body of President Lincoln from Washington to Springfield, a dramatic if morbid gesture to the man who had inspired the project.

The finale of this epic of railroad building was the famous gold spike ceremony, when the Central Pacific and the Union Pacific rails were joined on 10 May 1869 at Promontory Point in the desolate lands north of the Great Salt Lake. Two locomotives steamed slowly towards each other, Union Pacific's *No 119* and the Central Pacific *Jupiter,* until they gently touched. The engineers of each locomotive got down from their cabs and solemnly broke a bottle of champagne on each other's locomotive.

Trains which ran over immense distances encouraged American development of engines of greater fuel and water capacity and more tractive power. Thatcher Perkins, Master of Machinery at the Mount Clare workshops of the Baltimore and Ohio, gradually augmented the line's 4-4-0s with 4-6-0s to handle freight trains and the heavy expresses with 'hotel' cars, introduced by George Pullman in 1867.

In the same year the Lehigh Valley Railroad, created by the amalgamation of a number of companies, introduced massive 2-8-0s to handle its anthracite coal traffic. To mark the merger, the first of these engines was named *Consolidation,* which subsequently became the description of this wheel arrangement. A year after *Consolidation* the Lehigh Valley ordered *Decapod,* the worl's first ten-coupled engine.

Massive engines of these types impressed the developing countries, whose trade depended on the production and transportation of raw materials in bulk. In neighbouring Canada railway development had been slow. Apart from a 15-mile line built in 1836 between Laprairie, opposite Montreal, and St John's on Lake

below **A scene at the station at Omaha on the Pacific Railway.**

bottom **A Southern Pacific express hauled by a 4-4-0 unloads passengers to continue their journey by stage coach. By 1866 the Wells Fargo Co had the largest stage coach network in the United States and controlled almost all the services west of the Missouri river. The company gradually bought up rail routes and by 1888 owned a system which provided a complete transcontinental link.**

opposite page **An advertisement issued three months after the completion of the US transcontinental railroad. The remarkable power of the American 4-4-0 is exemplified if the illustration is accurate. Hauling a mail coach and four carriages up the slopes of the Sierra Nevada east of Sacramento, with a rise of nearly 3,000 feet over a distance of 25 miles, was no mean feat for any engine.**

SECOND CLASS TICKETS EASTWARD!

AUGUST, 1869.

CENTRAL PACIFIC R. R. OF CALIFORNIA.

SACRAMENTO to OMAHA, - - - $45 00 Coin.

Do.   " CHICAGO, - - - 45 00 "

Do.   " ST. LOUIS, - - - 45 00 "

Do.   " NEW YORK, - - 55 00 "

SECOND CLASS TRAIN

Leaves Sacramento Daily (Sundays excepted), at 2 o'clock P.M.

Ticket Office, at Passenger Depot,

SACRAMENTO.

below **A Thatcher-Perkins 4-6-0 locomotive of the Baltimore and Ohio Railroad.**

opposite, top *The Countess of Dufferin,* **named after the wife of the Deputy Governor General of Canada, was the first to work on the Canadian Pacific. A standard engine from the Baldwin Locomotive Works, it was built for Northern Pacific in 1872, and bought by the CPR in 1883. The line from west to east in Canada was completed in November, 1885, and**

the first transcontinental train left Montreal for Port Moody, British Columbia, on 28 June, 1886. The trip took 139 hours.

opposite, bottom *No 999,* **the most famous locomotive in US railroad history. This engine was the culmination of American know-how in building outside cylinder 4-4-0s, and hauled the crack express trains of the New York Central Railroad. On 10 May, 1893, it touched 112·5 mph near Batavia, New York State, on the straight track east of Buffalo.**

Champlain, and operated by a Stephenson engine, neither the British nor the French considered railway transportation an economic proposition in a sparsely populated country with formidable obstacles of distance, water, and mountains. By mid-century fewer than a hundred miles of Canadian track existed. The first major project linked Montreal with Portland, Maine, to provide an ice-free port during the winter. This link with the United States inevitably resulted in the use of American locomotives. The danger of the American Civil War to Canadian security resulted in a plan to build a strategic line from Montreal to Halifax. This was operated by both British and American engines.

The construction of the Canadian Pacific, linking the North Atlantic with the Pacific, created a promising market for United States locomotive builders. When the line was completed in 1885 some of the gradients necessitated the use of the most powerful engines available. In the Rocky Mountains it was normal to use four or six *Consolidation* 2-8-0s, and even then speed was only 5–6 mph.

Canada was an exception to railway development in other countries of the British Empire, where the vast majority of the lines were built by British engineers and their advice accepted as regards motive power. In Australia the first line was built with convict labour from Sydney to Parramata. Stephenson supplied its locomotive, delivered in September 1855.

The first locomotive in Asia, the British-made *Sultan,* steamed out of the station at Bombay for the neighbouring town of Thana. The date was 16 April 1853, the birth of a railway network which within a generation spanned the subcontinent and carried 100 million passengers a year, mainly with British locomotives. The political importance of India encouraged British makers to modify designs for the varied gauges of the Indian lines, and to develop heavy, powerful engines little used in Britain. Outside cylinder 4-6-0s

by North British and 2-8-0s from Stephenson ultimately became the standard types for main line work.

Railway hunger in the large and only partially industrialized nations was not easily satisfied. The three principal manufacturers of locomotives – Britain, Germany, and the United States – were so busy meeting the needs of their domestic markets that export trade was often rejected.

Typical of this problem was the experience of Russia. Some attempts had been made by Russian inventors to emulate British engineers as early as 1834 when the Cherepanovs, father and son, built a locomotive at their ironworks at Nizhnii Tagil in the Urals. It exploded during tests, but further models were said to be capable of hauling sixty tons.

The Austrian Von Gerstner, builder of the Danube-Moldavia line, proposed to the Czar a twenty-year monopoly on Russian railway construction. By 1838 a line was operating between St Petersburg (Leningrad) and Pavlovsk. The three engines came from England. One, *Rossiya,* was still running twenty years later.

When the Czar decided on a line to connect St Petersburg and Moscow, Russian engineers were sent to America in 1842 to study railroad and locomotive construction. They brought back J. Whistler, father of the artist, as technical adviser. As a result Americans were engaged to build and run a locomotive works with orders to build 162 engines. The first models were 0-6-0 freighters, built as simply as possible. Later a pair of leading wheels was added to improve weight distribution. For passenger trains the American engineers adopted their traditional 4-4-0 design, and in 1858 0-8-0s were introduced. In that year appeared a wheel arrangement never used before or since. To haul the royal train two 4-4-0s were modified with a pair of wheels in front of the bogie, thus making them 6-4-0s. The reason for this unusual arrangement was to minimize the risk of derailment should the engine meet any obstacle on the rails.

HIGH NOON OF STEAM

The potentialities of designing and building steam locomotives for overseas use resulted in an increasing divergence of manufacture in Britain. The large independent firms, such as North British Locomotive and Stephenson, built for foreign markets, particularly for countries in the Empire. In contrast, the major railway companies tended to build their own engines in their own shops, producing designs for a specific purpose and always with an eye to beating the competing line. This insularity was perhaps regrettable, but it did result in an enormous variety of designs, each marking progress which earned the sometimes grudging admiration of countries which did not enjoy the density of traffic to justify this specialized approach.

The great Crewe shops of the LNWR enhanced their reputation when Francis Webb, who as Ramsbottom's senior draughtsman had been closely concerned with the design and production of the *Newton* engines, took over as Chief Mechanical Engineer in 1871. Manufacture of *Newtons* continued while Webb worked on designs for his 2-4-0 *Precursor* and *Precedent* classes. The former were slightly larger versions of the *Newton,* with 5½-foot driving wheels. A larger boiler and firebox made them some 2¼ tons heavier.

The first *Precursor* ran in the spring of 1874. By the end of the year Webb had his first *Precedent* in service. The basic design was that of the *Newton* and *Precursor,* with an extra inch on the cylinder diameter and driving wheels of 6 feet 7½ inches. Small though these locomotives were, when compared with express motive power on other lines, they were big for the northern section of the LNWR, and their drivers called them *Jumbos,* a name which became better known than *Precedent.*

Forty *Precursor* engines were built, all eventually being converted to tank engines. The *Precedents* totalled seventy, and ninety-six of the *Newtons* were rebuilt as *Precedents* when they came into the shops for major overhaul. The individual names are redolent of railway history, either in their own right or as a nostalgic reference to past glories. Both *Rocket* and *Novelty* steamed once again on northern rails, and memorable, if unusual, names included *Caractacus, Wizard,* and *President Lincoln.*

Of all the names achieving immortality *Hardwicke* and *Vulcan* stand by themselves. In the 'Races to the North' in August 1888 *Vulcan* averaged 60 mph nonstop from Preston to Carlisle. When the rivalry with the GNR and NER was resumed in 1895, *Hardwicke* made the run from Crewe to Carlisle on the night of August 22–23 at an average of 67·2 mph start-to-stop. North of Shap the engine reached 85 to 90 mph for close on thirty miles.

Hardwicke has become a distinguished name among these superb little engines. More popular with the contemporary travelling public was *Charles Dickens,* one of the last of the class to be built, in 1882. For years it

below A *Precursor* of the LNWR, *No 513* was the first of this class, designed and completed by George Whale in ten months in 1903-04. Rarely has a locomotive, built straight off the drawing board, been such an immediate and unqualified success, and in three years 120 of these reliable engines went into service.

bottom *Hardwicke*, groomed and posed for a photo for posterity. This famous engine of the *Precedent* class of 2-4-0s, with their 6 feet 7½ inch coupled drivers, had capabilities of speed and power hardly obvious from their size and weight. *Hardwicke* gained fame during the races to the north in 1895, when it took the London-Aberdeen night express on the Crewe-Carlisle section at an average speed of 67 mph.

hauled the London-Manchester express, making the double trip every weekday with a record of timekeeping which became a byword both with passengers and the people who lived within sight or hearing of the line.

Somewhat similar to the *Precedent* was the *800* class on the Midland Railway. The London terminus of St Pancras had been opened in the autumn of 1868 and traffic thereupon became so heavy that the Kirtley 2-2-2s, known as the *Twenty-fives* from the number of the first one built in 1862, had often to be double-headed. Kirtley thereupon designed the *800* class of 2-4-0s. They were robust engines with cylinders of 17 by 24 inches, fed by steam at 140 pounds from a boiler with a total heating surface of 1,088 square feet. The driving wheels were 6 feet 8 inches. The need for these engines was urgent enough for Neilsons of Glasgow to help the Derby works with production. In the event the Scots firm made thirty of them, Derby supplying a further eighteen. The first *800* made its inaugural run in June 1870, a golden year for new and revolutionary locomotives.

Every historic steam locomotive has its devotees, but if there was a worldwide poll few engines could hope to rival the *Stirlings* as the best-loved machines ever to run on the world's rails. For the majority of people, the elegant, functional appearance is the appeal; for the enthusiast, their near-perfection as an example of engineering in the heyday of the steam locomotive.

Patrick Stirling had proved his genius as early as 1857 when, as the young locomotive superintendent at Kilmarnock on the Glasgow and South Western Railway, he began building outside-cylindered singles for fast working on a line which was regarded by the major English companies as merely a local system. The first well-known engine by Stirling, which was a modern

version of the outside-cylinder 2-2-2s built at Dundee in 1839 for the Arbroath and Forfar Railway, had driving wheels of 6½ feet in diameter. It remained a standard type on the line until 1865, and was the forerunner of the famous GNR engines. It had a domeless boiler with a heating surface of 1,165 square feet. The outside cylinders measured 18 by 28 inches. The weight was heavy – 38½ tons – which forced Stirling to adopt a leading bogie, an innovation which he would have avoided if the leading overhang had been lighter. This bogie had widely spaced wheels, 3 feet 11 inches in diameter (the trailing wheels were 4 feet 1 inch), and was a major factor in the steady running of a Stirling when driven hard. The superb distribution of weight meant that the driving wheels of 8 feet 1½ inch bore fifteen tons, a proportion which in practice proved perfect for adhesion. In the years 1870–95, fifty-three engines of this class were built, the last of them still under construction when Patrick Stirling died. The final version had larger cylinders, 19½ by 28 inches.

Stirling had taken over at the Doncaster works of the GNR in 1866. His first design was for a 2-2-2 express locomotive. The cylinders were 17 by 24 inches and the drivers 7 feet 1 inch. This was followed by a 2-4-0 version for use on stopping trains and for fast freight work. Both types were built between 1867–70. Stirling had therefore been working towards his masterpiece for a dozen years, testing ideas and improving on the basic design. In 1870 his patient work resulted in the emergence of *Stirling No 1* from the Doncaster works. When the *GNR No 1* went into service the 'Special Scotch Express', as the Flying Scotsman was then known, took 10½ hours for the journey from London to Edinburgh. Route improvements and the *Stirling* performance cut this time to 9 hours by 1876. During the dramatic weeks of the 1895 'Races to the North', *Stirling No 668* covered the 105½ miles from King's Cross to Grantham in 101 minutes; *No 775* then took over and reached York, 82¾ miles distant, in 76 minutes. The climax of the contest between the east and west routes came for the GNR on the night of August 21–22, 1895, when the sleeper express covered the 393 miles from King's Cross to Edinburgh in 6 hours 19 minutes, which was proof of Stirling's magnificent design, though an example of reckless running.

A Scots contemporary of Stirling, William Stroudley, had his countryman's gift for implanting his own personality on the engines he designed. He began to learn his trade on the footplate, and all his life he was a practical engineer, not a theorist. His first important

opposite, top **A** *Precedent* **in working fettle outside the sheds:** *No 883 Phantom.* **Large cylinders, a large boiler, high steam pressure, and a short steam flow to the cylinders were among Webb's innovations which made these engines so much in advance of their time.**

opposite, bottom **A Midland Railway 0-6-0 designed by Matthew Kirtley. This class of locomotive became the standard freight type, and the Midland, with plenty of mineral traffic, was to the forefront in using these powerful engines, notably those Kirtley introduced in 1878.**

below **One of the** *800* **class express locomotives used by the Midland Railway for the Anglo-Scottish service. Originally to a Kirtley design, the** *800s* **were modernized by S. W. Johnson after 1875 with larger boilers and cylinders. Forty-eight were built at Derby and Glasgow, and most were still busy after fifty years of hard work.**

bottom **The first Stirling eight-footer, built at Doncaster in 1870 and now preserved at York. Stirling was engineer, craftsman, and artist – and his talents all evident in these beautiful and functional engines. Fifty-three were at work by 1895, pulling the fastest trains in the world, including a record run in that year with the night sleeper express for Aberdeen, covering London to Grantham (105½ miles) in 101 minutes.**

position, in 1865, was as locomotive superintendent of the Highland Railway. Five years later he moved to the London, Brighton and South Coast Railway, ruling its locomotive department with a rod of iron till his death in 1889. As had been his policy at Inverness, rebuilding engines already in service was his first task at Brighton. Then he designed a small and powerful engine for the London suburban services, where commuter traffic, although lucrative, was becoming difficult. Stroudley's *Terrier* tank engines were 0-6-0s weighing 24 tons. The cylinders of 13 by 28 inches drove coupled wheels of 4-foot diameter, and steam pressure was 140 pounds. Twentieth-century Londoners, whose main reaction to their train services is to grumble about delays and overcrowding, can have little conception of the affection the Victorian commuters afforded to these handsome little engines, always kept in perfect conditions with their greenish-yellow livery (dubbed daffodil by the public), the copper-capped chimney, and the neat lining out. Stroudley, dour and practical as he was, recognized the value of names in enhancing the interest of engine crews and passengers. All fifty *Terriers* built between 1872–80 were given names to arouse local interest. Most were named after the stations they served: *Tulse Hill, Clapham, Tooting, Peckham,* and so on. Those kept for local trains in the southern section were called by such names as *Crowborough* and *Southdown.* One of these engines, *Brighton,* was selected for display at the Paris Exposition of 1878; it wore the gold medal awarded to it for the rest of its service life.

Stroudley had authorized the Paris exhibit for more practical motives than gaining prestige. Anxious to obtain more of the continental traffic by developing the Newhaven-Dieppe route, he wanted the Western Rail-

way of France to improve their snail-like service to Paris. This was a difficult and poorly constructed line, and an average of 40 mph for the 105-mile run was considered by the French to be impossible. A *Terrier* was loaned. With a standard train of French coaches it easily reached 50 mph, which meant sales of *Terriers* in France. The *Brighton* was eventually sold to the Isle of Wight Central Railway, where it became *No 11.*

Stroudley also built 0-4-2 tank engines for fast freight trains. Their main job was hauling inter-continental freight shipped via Newhaven, and they were named after towns and tourist centres in Europe, the class usually being known as *Lyons,* after the first one to go into service. From 1876–78 these engines had cylinders of 17 by 24 inches and driving wheels of 5½ feet. A rather heavier version made from 1878–80 had cylinders of 17¼ by 26 inches and driving wheels of 6½ feet.

Stroudley's supreme design was undoubtedly the *Gladstone* class, the first of thirty-six appearing in 1882. It had cylinders of 18¼ by 26 inches, coupled wheels of 6½ feet and weighed 38¾ tons. A notable feature was the reversing gear, operated by compressed air supplied through the braking system (perfected in the United States by George Westinghouse in 1869), and curious but evidently effective aids to smooth running were vents to direct exhaust steam against the flanges of the foremost driving wheels to act as a lubricant. The long service which these engines gave was largely due to the robust specifications insisted on by Stroudley and the meticulous maintenance he instituted, but an additional reason was that the driver 'owned' the engine. On appointment to one, he worked it and no other while he remained in the railway's service and his name was painted in the cab. The original *Gladstone, No 214,*

worked until 1927, by which time it had completed an estimated 1,370,000 miles.

The Scottish influence on locomotive design in the closing years of the nineteenth century was strengthened by the work of the brothers Drummond. The elder, Dugald Drummond, had been a foreman at Inverness when Stroudley was in charge of the Highland Railway locomotives. He came south as manager of the Brighton works until, in 1875, he moved to the North British Railway, Scotland's largest railway system. At the outset the Drummonds (the younger brother Peter worked with Dugald at this period) used the basic Stroudley designs for express engines and tankers, but in 1876 the first notable Drummond 4-4-0 express locomotive was built. Many of the Stroudley ideas were again adopted, but his dislike of a leading bogie was rejected. The 9-foot base of the 6½-foot coupled wheels gave room for a large, long firebox, and the heating surface of 1,193 square feet produced steam at a working pressure of 150 pounds. These powerful engines, named after places on the North British system, hauled the passenger expresses from London on the final stage from Carlisle to Edinburgh. The trains included the heavy Pullman coaches just introduced from the United States. The *Drummond* engines' impressive performance over this difficult line resulted in the 4-4-0 type becoming a normal feature of express running all over the country, not least because the Drummond brothers changed jobs frequently and took their policy to each new appointment. From the North British they transferred to the Caledonian, where the North British type, with minor changes, became the standard express engine. In the races of 1895 one of these *Drummond* 4-4-0s, *No 90,* ran from Carlisle to Perth at a start-to-stop speed of 60 mph.

In 1896 the Drummond brothers took separate posts, Peter as locomotive superintendent of the Highland Railway and Dugald with the LSWR. At Inverness Peter Drummond succeeded David Jones, who had started as a locomotive foreman twenty-six years before. Jones had been responsible for many highly successful designs, beginning with the *F* class of 4-4-0s in 1874, the largest passenger engines of their day. They are usually known as the *Duke* locomotives, after the best known, *Duke of Sutherland.* Others in the class were named after Scottish shires, but during their operation these fine locomotives' names were regularly, and confusingly, altered and exchanged from one engine to another. By the late eighties, trains taken over from the south were becoming much heavier, and Jones produced an entirely new design: the first 4-6-0 in Britain. The first of the 'Jones Goods' was ready in September 1894. They were built in seven months, without preliminary tests, and relying entirely on Jones' design; when the first one made its inaugural run there were another fourteen nearing completion. Two years later came the 4-4-0 *Loch* class, a simple and workmanlike engine with outside cylinders. When a railside accident cut short this outstanding engineer's career he had completed the design for the *Castle* class of 4-6-0s.

The trend towards standardization of design was growing, though understandably it was a controversial subject with every major railway, each employing highly individualistic designers, whose views on rationalization concerned the particular requirements of their own traffic. Rising costs and line amalgamations encouraged this sensible if unglamorous policy. There was also the example set by the American standardization policy pioneered by the splendidly named

Master of Machinery for the Pennsylvania Railroad, Alexander J Cassatt. The basic locomotive designs were prepared under his supervision at the Altoona works.

The first British versions of the successful United States *Mogul* (2-6-0) locomotive, with an impressive record on the Pennsylvania Railroad, had appeared in 1878 on the Great Eastern Railway. They were designed by William Adams, who joined the GER in 1873. Many of the features of his outside cylinder engine were copied from America. Altogether fifteen were built, mostly by Massey Bromley, who took over when Adams left the GER to take charge of locomotives on the LSWR in 1878. The GER *Moguls* were not successful, owing to trouble with the unfamiliar American valve arrangement. Bromley might well have ironed out these initial difficulties, but he was killed in the notorious railway accident which occurred at Penistone in 1884.

This major disaster, caused by the fracture of a crank axle, also brought to an end the career of another notable engineer, Charles Sacré, locomotive chief of the Manchester, Sheffield and Lincolnshire Railway. In 1877 he began building 4-4-0 engines, designed to haul heavy expresses over the notorious Pennine gradients and to run fast on the easy stretches. The fracture of the axle at Penistone might not have caused too serious a derailment but for the fact that the train was equipped with a vacuum brake invented by J. Y. Smith, machine superintendent with the United States Military Railroads Department. However, Sacré, a sensitive and emotional Frenchman, regarded the accident as his responsibility and resigned from the MS & LR. He later committed suicide.

opposite, top **A veteran of the *Iron Duke* class. The first was built at Swindon to Daniel Gooch's design in 1847. The photo of *Alma* was taken in 1888 by which time the class had been modernized: wood lagging on the boiler removed, and a cab added. These engines were the mainstay of the GWR express services until the broad gauge was abolished in 1892.**

opposite, bottom **William Stroudley's small *Terrier* tank engines, reliable, powerful, and virtually indestructible, were built to handle the heavy suburban traffic in the south London suburbs. Fifty of the 0-6-0s went into service after** 1872; a rather larger version with an 0-4-2 wheel arrangement handled stopping trains all over the London-Brighton system.

below **A *Gladstone* in honourable museum retirement. This famous class was introduced by Stroudley in 1882. Thirty-six of them worked the busy routes from London to the Sussex coast, handling very heavy loads in holiday periods. The first engine, shown here, was retired in 1927 after forty-five years' service.**

bottom **a Drummond 'Small Ben' 4-4-0,** *Ben Slioch.*

below **A German** *DB* **class** *38* 4-6-0 *No 553* **hauling a morning train near Schiltach.**

bottom **The LMS Pacific,** *Princess Elizabeth,* **one of a fine class designed by Stanier in 1933.**

opposite, top **An original German** *01* **Pacific 4-6-2, photographed near Marktschorgast.**

opposite, bottom **A narrow gauge Garratt at Port Elizabeth, South Africa.**

COMPOUNDS & SUPERHEATERS

After 1875 locomotive engineers in many European countries developed ideas aimed at securing fuel economy by making better use of the steam produced. Anatole Mallet's compound engine, with one high pressure cylinder and another using the steam at low pressure, was introduced on the Bayonne-Biarritz Railway in 1876. Mallet-type engines, usually tankers, were soon running on different lines, such as the Central Railway in Switzerland.

Then, in 1885, A. G. de Glehn designed his famous four-cylinder compound, with two inside high pressure cylinders and two outside low pressure cylinders. In 1891 this system was modified by G. du Bousquet, locomotive chief of the Nord line of France, by interchanging the high and low pressure cylinders and coupling the driving wheels. The engines built on this principle became a European type. In France the most famous were *Les Grands Chocolats,* 4-4-0s, followed in

the 1890s by 4-4-2s on the Nord line and in 1908 by 4-6-0s. The last were very numerous, their flexibility enabling them to haul expresses at 70 mph or a thousand-ton freight train at a steady 21 mph, in both cases with more fuel economy than any engine of its size.

In Britain coal was plentiful and cheap, so the compound idea was largely of mere theoretical interest. But F. W. Webb of the LNWR, perpetually preoccupied on his directors' orders with cutting costs, used the Mallet system to modify a 2-2-2 Allan engine. Performance was good enough to make Webb an enthusiastic advocate of the compound locomotive. In 1882 appeared his first compounds, the *Experiment* class. The description is the exceptional one of 2-2-2-0. The two pairs of driving wheels were uncoupled, a single low pressure inside cylinder, 26 by 24 inches, connected to the foremost driving wheels, and two outside cylinders of $11\frac{1}{2}$ by 26 inches to the rear drivers. Webb's reason for

below **An engraving of** *Greater Britain,* **a 2-(2-2)-2 introduced by F. W. Webb on the LNWR in 1892. The leading drivers were connected to the low pressure cylinder and the trailing drivers to a pair of high pressure cylinders.** *Greater Britain* **hauled the ceremonial train during Queen Victoria's diamond jubilee journeys during 1897.**

leaving the wheels uncoupled was that he believed he would obtain smooth running and greater efficiency through a decrease in friction. It was true enough that the *Experiment* cruised well when the cylinders were perfectly synchronized, but this was by no means frequent.

There was undoubtedly an improvement in the use of available steam, and consequent fuel economy, which could always be relied on to impress the LNWR directors. With some modifications, a further twenty-nine *Experiment* class engines were built. Then in 1884 came the *Dreadnought* class, of which the best known was *Marchioness of Stafford.* Drivers were 6 feet 3 inches and the low pressure and high pressure cylinders were enlarged to 30 and 14 inches as compared with the *Experiments.* These were followed by the *Teutonic* class, with an improved valve gear and driving wheels of 7 feet 1 inch. Ten of these engines were built in 1889–90,

and were by far the best of a rather disappointing series. Their names were linked with the White Star steamship line, being given names similar to the company's liners, *Pacific, Ionic, Adriatic,* etc. After Webb's retirement in 1903 little effort was made to maintain the three classes of Webb compound express engines, and by 1907 they had all been rebuilt or broken up.

In Germany, partly as a result of research into marine engines, A. von Borries designed a two-cylinder compound locomotive in 1880 in which the cylinders were of nearly the same size. The driver had control over the use of high pressure steam in the low pressure cylinder so that on starting the engine could be worked as a non-compound.

This system was adopted by Thomas Worsdell on the Great Eastern Railway in 1884. In the previous two years he had built some 2-4-0 locomotives with 18 by 24 inch cylinders and 7-foot driving wheels, and these

below *Oliver Cromwell,* **a 4-6-2** *Britannia* **class locomotive, pounding along Giggleswick Bank.**

bottom **The original oil-fired express engine,** *Petrolea,* **GER class** *T 19,* **built in 1890. The Great Eastern Railway had got into trouble for river pollution, and a good way of disposing of the effluent was to burn it in the engines. The** *Petrolea,* **designed by James Holden, proved a successful answer to the pollution problem.**

opposite page **An ex-War Department 2-8-0** *Austerity* **locomotive.**

gave him the basic design for his compounds. The low pressure cylinder was enlarged to a 26-inch diameter, and the leading single axle replaced with a bogie. Eleven of these engines were built, and although records showed that fuel saving amounted to 14 per cent, as compared with the consumption on the earlier and more simple engines, they were phased out after Worsdell left the GER to join the North Eastern at the end of 1885. He then began the construction of compound engines for every kind of traffic which the NER handled. First came the *D* class of 2-4-0s, soon modified with a front bogie as Class *F*. One of these, *No 1324,* was exhibited at Newcastle during the Jubilee celebrations of 1887 alongside the 1825 *Locomotion* as an example of progress in locomotive engineering.

Worsdell was constantly introducing improvements, with the new type duly being given an alphabetical classification. Of special interest were the *I* and *J* classes of 4-2-2s introduced from 1889–90. The main difference was drivers of 7 feet 1 inch on the former and 7 feet 7 inches on the latter. These engines were fast, reliable and economical, but were not powerful enough for the heavy expresses this line had to handle. Restrictions on space between the frame for the inside cylinder and the structural gauge limitations as regards outside cylinders prevented Worsdell giving them a greater capacity. When he retired (the post was kept in the family, with the appointment of Wilson Worsdell) the *I* and *J* classes were converted to simple engines.

Experiments with compound engines were worldwide during this period. Notable was the four-cylinder engine built in 1885 in France by A. G. de Glehn, in which two high pressure inside cylinders drove one pair of wheels and two low pressure outside cylinders drove a second pair. The idea was improved in 1891 by G. du Bousquet, with cylinders which could be changed as regards pressure, and the driving wheels were coupled. This system was widely adapted on European railways for heavy 4-6-0s. Its rival for international recognition was the Vauclain compound patent of 1889, adopted by the Baldwin locomotive plant in the United States. It had the merit of mechanical simplicity: the two outside cylinders were double, a high pressure one above the low pressure piston. The adjacent rods were connected to a single crosshead.

These innovations failed to persuade Webb of the LNWR to alter his opinion on the advantages of his three-cylinder compounds. In 1891 the *Greater Britain* class went into service. They looked impressive with their long boilers, in which there was a combustion chamber mid-way. Steam pressure was 175 pounds. Performance was not really better than that of the *Teutonics,* but the class became very well known, Webb using them to celebrate the Diamond Jubilee of 1897 by painting one of them red, another white, and a third blue. The white one, *Queen Empress,* was sent to the United States and ran on Illinois tracks as part of the publicity campaign for the Chicago Exposition.

below A French Pacific of the Paris, Lyon, and Mediterranean Railway. The original engines, built between 1909-12, had a simple four-cylinder power system; many were rebuilt as compounds after 1925. They maintained express services until the end of steam on French railways.

bottom No C-127, built at Arles in 1900 for the Paris, Lyon, and Mediterranean Railway. This class of 4-4-0s owed much to American design, and 120 of them were built in different French shops.

right **Daniel Gooch poses for his portrait in 1888, a year before his death at the age of 73. He had then completed fifty years' service with the GWR. A baronetcy was conferred in 1866 in recognition of his work on the transatlantic cable. His death was said to have been hastened when he had to accept that his broad gauge system was doomed.**

Jubilee **class** *No 45562, Alberta.*

A Neilson tank locomotive built by Neilson and Co in 1876. This firm had a large business in robust little engines for work in freight yards and on narrow gauge lines.

Only ten of these locomotives were built. They were succeeded after 1897 by Webb's *Black Prince* class, in which he finally abandoned the three-cylinder concept for a four-cylinder compound. The outside high pressure cylinders were 15 inches in diameter and the inside low pressure cylinders 19½ inches, all four in line beneath the smokebox. Steam pressure was 200 pounds. Forty were built over three years, and a further forty with an improved valve gear between 1901–3. As happened with so many of these later LNWR compounds, many of them were subsequently converted to simple engines.

In this golden era of the steam locomotive, innovation and experiment were the watchwords of the engineers, who enjoyed the power and prestige of virtually unquestioned control of a railway's motive power. In those cases where a long company tradition was prone to inhibit enterprise, circumstances inevitably enforced change. This was the case with the GWR. For years the line had justifiably relied on the Gooch singles to maintain its reputation for running the fastest regular services in the world. But remorselessly the Brunel broad gauge was disappearing, mile by mile, over a period of twenty-four years, until, in May 1892, the last engine was converted in the Swindon shops.

After Gooch's retirement, William Dean, the GWR locomotive superintendent, was responsible for the design of the convertible engines. In 1891 he completed a new 2-2-2 with inside cylinders of 20 by 24 inches and driving wheels of 7 feet 8 inches. No one could design an engine in which most of the parts below the boiler were temporary which looked anything but clumsy, but this ugly duckling emerged as a standard gauge beauty when Dean changed the wheel arrangement to 4-2-2. These engines were immediately successful and by the end of the century eighty were busy restoring GWR prestige. Many of these locomotives took over the names of the old Gooch singles, such as *North Star* and *Lord of the Isles*. Others were given names redolent of the West Country: *Westward Ho!, Lorna Doone, Devonia,* and *White Horse*. The champion of the class was *Duke of Connaught,* which, in May 1904, took over the up ocean mail from Plymouth and ran from Bristol to Paddington at an average of 71·3 mph, including seventy miles between Shrivenham and Westbourne Park at an average of 80 mph. This was a light train of four mail and baggage vans. For express passenger work in the new century, heavier locomotives were needed; the day of the single driver, holder of speed records all over the country, was ending, though in the final phase other companies ran some notable examples.

An outstanding engine appeared on the Midland Railway, which paradoxically had never been very enthusiastic about the single driver until other lines were abandoning it. The reason for this belated regard was that the Midland's locomotive superintendent, S. W. Johnson, was impressed with the efficiency of a steam sander devised at the Derby works. If this sander could obviate the serious lack of adhesion when a single driver started, and minimize the imperceptible slipping during normal running, then the advantages of the type would outweigh its disadvantages for light, fast trains. To test the sander, coupling rods were removed from some Midland 4-4-0s. As singles they ran faster on the level and were at least equal to the coupled engine on gradients. The first of the Johnson 4-2-2s came out in 1887, and a larger version between 1889–93. The drivers were 7 feet 9 inches, and the inside cylinders 19½ by 26 inches. The best known was *Princess of Wales,* which impressed the French when exhibited at the Paris Exposition of 1900 among all the coupled engines claiming to represent the modern trend.

In the 1890s there were some handsome new 4-2-2s on the GER. They were built on the orders of James Holden, who succeeded Thomas Worsdell when the latter moved to the NER. Holden's idea was to have a range of powerful engines for fast non-stop running between London and the Norfolk towns, and to make them oil burners. The first of his *No 10* class of single drivers began working the Liverpool Street-Cromer expresses in 1896. They were followed by the *Claud Hamilton* class, powerful 4-4-0s introduced in 1900. Basically they were of the same design as the singles they replaced, but with a larger boiler and cylinders.

Holden was a champion of the steam locomotive and always insisted that it was unsurpassed both on the grounds of economy and efficiency. With his assistant, Fred Russell, he designed a steam locomotive to compete with electric traction. The *Decapod* was a ten-coupled tank engine with three cylinders of 18½ by 24 inches, capable of reaching 30 mph in thirty seconds. It is regrettable that this unique engine was not preserved, if only as an example of specialization. After four years in service it was rebuilt as an 0-8-0 and used for freight haulage.

The GNR, already famous for its superb singles, enhanced its reputation in 1898 with the Atlantic, the first 4-4-2 of its type built in Britain. At first it had only a number, *990,* but later was named *Henry Oakley* and is one of the notables in railway history. The designer, Harry Ivatt, came to the GNR after the death of Patrick Stirling. Ivatt had previously been in charge of locomotives on the Great Southern and Western Railway of Ireland. He was a very cautious engineer, prepared to study the traffic requirements on a system very different from that in Ireland before he authorized construction of a new type of locomotive. His Atlantics were needed to haul expresses weighing as much as 300 tons–twice the weight that the Stirling singles had originally handled. The new engine weighed 58 tons, and the distribution of weight over the coupled wheels of 6 feet 7½ inches gave first rate adhesion. The outside cylinders were 18¾ by 24 inches fed by steam at 175 pounds from a boiler with a heating surface nearly half as much again as in a Stirling.

Either by coincidence or through friendly rivalry, an Atlantic was put on the Lancashire and Yorkshire Railway less than a year later. The planning and design had been simultaneous. The L & Y engine was the work of John Aspinall, who had preceded Ivatt on the Irish line, the men becoming friends during the changeover period. Aspinall's need was for a locomotive which could accelerate quickly on routes with frequent stops, and maintain speed on the many gradients in the Pennines. Generally, L & Y trains were not heavy, but the Aspinall Atlantics were rather more powerful than those of the GNR. They had inside cylinders of 19 by 26 inches and coupled wheels of 7¼ feet. Their performance was magnificent, putting the L & Y in the forefront of fast passenger services. On the Manchester-Liverpool route of thirty-six miles they were given schedules necessitating regular bursts of 85 and 90 mph, and enthusiastic passengers claimed that 100 mph was not unusual according to the admittedly rather unreliable stop watch timing.

In terms of power these L & Y engines had the edge on Ivatt's Atlantics which were soon expected to haul expresses of a weight Ivatt could hardly have envisaged when he began his design. Passengers' demands for increased comfort resulted, in 1900, in the introduction of American-style 12-wheeled coaches. On long-distance expresses there were restaurant and sleeping cars. Each coach could weigh as much as forty tons, and a well-patronized train such as the Flying Scotsman consisted of twelve such coaches. To handle this sort of load, Ivatt introduced a larger boilered Atlantic in 1901. At 2,500 square feet this locomotive had more than twice the heating surface of the Stirling single, and the firegrate area was 50 per cent larger. The first of this class was numbered *251.*

The value of increasing the size of boilers, so immediately effective when the new series of LNER locomotives came into service, had been demonstrated six years before on the Caledonian Railway, where John McIntosh produced the famous *Dunalastair* class. McIntosh had risen from the ranks, starting in the sheds, working as a driver, and subsequently as a locomotive inspector. For his engine he used the basic design of his predecessor Drummond, adding a bigger boiler 4 feet 8 inches in diameter, and with a steam pressure of 180 pounds. The first of the class, numbered *721,* was running in 1896 and took the heavy expresses from Carlisle to Stirling at an average speed of 57 mph.

Five of these *Dunalastairs* were also built for the Belgian State Railways, and were subsequently copied at the locomotive works at Liège. Belgium, and to a lesser extent Holland, were the only European countries to give a virtual monopoly to British firms, their small size and dense traffic being a close replica of British conditions. Elsewhere the French compounds shared building with Germany. The latter were producing a variety of interesting innovations.

The Atlantic was introduced to European railways in 1898 by Krauss of Munich for the Palatinate Railway. Six of them maintained the express services between Rotterdam and Basle, and Berling and Strasbourg. *Neuffer* was the best known of this class, which had inside cylinders of 19¼ by 22½ inches, and driving wheels of 6 feet 6 inches diameter. The smokebox and cab were conical to minimize wind resistance. More powerful Atlantics were introduced on the Baden State Railways in 1902 for expresses running between Mannheim and Oldenburg. At the time they were the most powerful locomotives built outside America.

Quite the most remarkable steam locomotive built at this period in Germany–or indeed anywhere–was a 4-4-4 with three compound cylinders. Designed by the Ministry of Public Works in Berlin, and built by Henschel of Cassel, the engine was completely sheathed

right **The first British Atlantic class designed by H. A. Ivatt in 1903. The original engine, *No 990,* was named Henry Oakley, after the general manager of the GNR. *No 1450,* shown here, was built in 1908.**
below **W. Dean's *City* class for the GWR were intended to compete with the LSWR on the lucrative express services on the London-Plymouth route.**
bottom **A Maffei 4-4-4 German engine which first ran on the Munich-Augsburg line in 1907. Maffei's chief engineer, Anton Hammel, broke new ground with this unusual wheel arrangement.**

from the streamlined driving cab at the front to the rear of the tender. Passages on each side within the sheathing gave entry to the corridor of the coaches. The object was to test the maximum speed and haulage capacity which could be embodied in a steam-propelled engine. The great success of European compound engines built on the de Glehn principle impressed George Churchward, who succeeded Dean as locomotive superintendent on the GWR in 1902. Churchward had designed the *City* class of 4-4-0s, which ran fast with light loads; a notable record was 102·3 mph in May 1904 with a short train carrying United States mail and bullion. But for heavy expresses, more powerful engines were needed. Churchward arranged to buy three French four-cylinder compound 4-4-2s for trials. The first French engine arrived in 1903 and was named *La France.* In the next two years two rather larger engines, *Alliance* and *President,* were imported. All three proved excellent engines, beautifully balanced and, thanks to the divided drive, they were smooth and steady runners at speed. They were, however, complicated to drive and maintain.

For the British entry in these trials Churchward used several of his two-cylinder simple 4-6-0s, including a modified engine, *No 171,* and named *Albion* when it was matched against *La France.* In order to make comparison of starting efficiency and general haulage power *Albion* was subsequently changed to a 4-4-2. It still compared favourably with the French engine.

For tests against the two more powerful French engines, Churchward used the general design of the 4-4-2 *Albion,* but installed four cylinders instead of two. It was given the most renowned name in GWR history: *North Star.* Its performance was such that any idea of buying more French compounds was abandoned. *North Star* heralded the famous series of *Star* engines. The first of these 4-6-0s (*North Star* was rebuilt after her trials as an Atlantic) appeared in 1907, and was named *Dog Star.* Nine more were completed in the same year. Not many pieces of machinery earn the description of masterpiece, but by general consent this is merited by the *Stars.*

Development of the design continued year by year, each new batch having its own class name; *Stars, Knights, Kings, Queens, Princes and Princesses;* the *Kings* were superheaters. By 1914 there were sixty of these magnificent engines, hauling expresses non-stop to Exeter at an average of 58 mph, or along the Cornish Riviera non-stop to Plymouth.

Not even Churchward's expertise could have envisaged the success of these engines; while the first were under construction he had completed his design for the first Pacific tender locomotive to be built for use in Britain. *The Great Bear* was ready in 1908. It would be unjust to brand it a failure but the fact remains that its designer's intention that the boiler and fuel capacity would enable it to take heavy expresses to the Cornish

resorts was brought to nothing by the permanent way engineers. They could not approve a huge locomotive weighing 97¼ tons running at speed on the lines west of Bristol. *The Great Bear* was therefore restricted to working expresses for which Churchward's 4-6-0s were perfectly adequate. Nevertheless, the locomotive was a splendid example of Swindon engineering expertise. Its four cylinders were 15 by 26 inches, driving coupled wheels of 6 feet 8½ inches. The tapered boiler barrel was 13 feet long–9 feet more than on the 4-6-0s–and had a heating surface of 2,831 square feet. Steam pressure was 225 pounds. It is a pity that this unique example of GWR engineering has not been preserved, but in 1924 it was

left A 4-6-0 class *Ub* built by Baldwin of Philadelphia for New Zealand Railways in the South Island, and operating by 1898. Weighing 57 tons, it was an unusually large engine for the difficult and hilly routes of the country.

below In 1908 Churchward built Britain's first 4-6-2, the only Pacific type seen in the country until 1922. Its weight and length confined it to the London-Bristol main line, and in 1924 it was rebuilt as a 4-6-0, *Viscount Churchill*, but retaining the original number, *111*. The photo was taken at a celebration centenary run.

rebuilt as a 4-6-0 and renamed *Viscount Churchill*.

The reliability of a well-designed simple engine, so spectacularly proven on the GWR, was reflected on the LNWR. Webb retired in 1903. With him disappeared his devotion to the compound principle. His successor, George Whale, needed scores of new engines. In a matter of weeks the design for a large-boiler 4-4-0 with inside cylinders was completed. The first of 120 of these engines, *Precursor,* was running by May 1904. Each week another was completed, and at times the output rose to one every three days.

At this period another resourceful engineer came to the fore. John G. Robinson learned his profession at the GWR Swindon works under Joseph Armstrong and William Dean, his career encouraged by his father, who was locomotive engineer of the Bristol-Exeter division. Robinson's first important post was on the Waterford, Limerick and Western Railway in Ireland. He was appointed to the Great Central Railway in 1900, a year after that line reached London.

The locomotives designed by Robinson were without doubt the best looking engines of the decade, and their beauty was more than skin deep. Many features were technically in advance of anything else being manufactured in quantity at the time. First came some 4-4-0s, which caused little comment beyond a growing reputation for maintaining a 55–60 mph schedule for the main line services with clockwork regularity. Then, in 1903, came the first of the GCR Atlantics, with outside cylinders of $19\frac{1}{2}$ by 16 inches and coupled driving wheels of $6\frac{3}{4}$ feet. Their enthusiastic crews dubbed them 'Lilies', the byword for beauty at a time when Lily Langtry was regarded as the loveliest woman on the London stage. 'Forward', the company's motto, was painted on engine and tender on the dark green livery, set off by the rich red underframes.

Two years later Robinson built four Atlantic compounds using the three-cylinder Smith system with divided drive. These were later fitted with superheaters. In 1907 came Robinson's formidable three-cylinder 0-8-4 shunting tank engines. The cylinders were 18 by 26 inches driving 4 foot 8 inch coupled wheels. Painted in workmanlike black, they still had the Robinson touch of glamour in their attractive lines.

A forceful management and the efficiency of the Robinson locomotives put the GCR on the main line map, with vastly increased passenger and freight traffic. The Atlantics were gradually replaced after 1913 by powerful 4-4-0s, the *Director* class, being used for both passenger and freight work. The crack expresses were handled by 4-6-0s, superheater engines with a heating surface of 2,377 square feet and inside cylinders of $21\frac{1}{2}$ by 26 inches, driving wheels of 6 feet 9 inches. Two-cylinder and four-cylinder versions of these 4-6-0s were produced. One of the best known was *Valour,* the memorial engine for GCR employees who died in the First World War.

left A Robinson *ROD* (Railway Operating Division) 2-8-0. The first engines of this class were introduced on the GCR in 1911. On the outbreak of war in 1914 the Government adopted the design for military locomotives, and more than 500 of them operated in Britain, France, and the Middle East. They returned to civilian work after 1918, and a few survived to contribute to the war effort in 1939-45.

below Collett's *King* class of 4-6-0s for the GWR were a development of the *Castle* class, and were the most powerful engines of their type in Britain. *King George V* was the first to be built and was shipped to the USA for the centenary celebrations of the Baltimore and Ohio Railroad.

The continuing stream of new locomotives, and modified versions of them, which Robinson designed was dominated as regards numbers by the 2-8-0 freight engines, first built in 1911. They had outside cylinders of 21 by 26 inches, driving the third pair of coupled wheels. This massive engine was selected by the Railway Operating Department of the War Office for military service overseas. Apart from taking over existing

GCR engines (as well as some from all the large companies) 541 were built to Government order. They worked munition, troop and general supply trains behind the front lines in France and the Middle East. After the Armistice many of these GCR *RODs* were shipped home and were put to work on all the main lines, a few again going overseas 'on active service' in 1939–45.

It will have been noted that the final versions of the GWR *Stars* and GCR Atlantics were superheated, one of the important improvements after 1900. The advantages of drying steam for increasing power while maintaining the same boiler pressure or even reducing it, with a consequent saving in fuel and increase in boiler life, had long been realized. By 1897 smokebox superheaters were in use on both United States and British engines. The fire tube superheater was invented in 1899 by Wilhelm Schmidt and used on 4-4-0s and 2-6-0s built for the Prussian State Railways. The economy achieved

in water consumption made superheaters attractive in arid countries and for use over long distances without sources of water. An early Schmidt superheater built in Britain was the class of 4-6-0s built by the North British Locomotive Co for the Cape Government Railways of South Africa. These engines were in operation in 1903.

In Britain experiments were made in 1906 on the GWR and the Lancashire and Yorkshire Railway, but the first practical development came two years later with ten tank engines, built by Douglas Earle-Marsh for the LBSCR. Their great success influenced C. J. Bowen-Cooke, appointed LNWR locomotive chief in 1908, to build two superheater classes. *King George the Fifth*, a 4-4-0, was completed in 1910, and a 4-6-0, *Prince of Wales*, in the following year. Both classes were mass produced, 245 *Prince of Wales* 4-6-0s being built over a period of twelve years. They were followed by Bowen-Cooke's *Claughton* class of 4-6-0s. The most famous of these engines was *Ralph Brocklebank*.

BIGGER & FASTER

In the two decades before the first World War the United States could claim not only the most powerful, but among the fastest, locomotives in the world. The traditional American express engine, the 4-4-0, appeared in its finest version in 1893, with a design by William Buchanan, motive power superintendent of the New York Central, and was used on the road's crack expresses, notably the *Empire State* from New York to Chicago. The best known was *No 999*. On 10 May 1893 it reached 112·5 mph near Batavia, New York a feat commemorated on a 2-cent United States Mail stamp.

The 4-4-0s were subsequently augmented by four-cylinder compound 4-4-2s, permitting a larger firebox and consequently better steaming. Their reliability became a byword. They hauled the *Twentieth Century Limited,* which first ran on 15 June 1902, on its 20-hour schedule for the 961 miles between New York and Chicago. Passengers were guaranteed a dollar refund for every hour the train was late. It very rarely had to be paid. This famous train, and its competitor, Pennsylvania's *Broadway Limited,* steadily brought the time down to seventeen hours by 1935.

The 4-4-2 design had been pioneered in the United States by Baldwins for the Philadelphia and Reading Railroad, which wanted fast, powerful engines for its Atlantic City Fliers. They were built on the compound system patented in 1889 by Baldwins' S. M. Vauclain, in which a high pressure cylinder and a low pressure cylinder beneath it on the outer sides of the frames worked piston rods fixed to a single crosshead, thus dispensing with additional mechanism to drive the wheels. These engines hauled trains from Camden, New Jersey, to Atlantic City at an average of 66 mph, involving very heavy loads at peak vacation periods. They were unusual looking machines, with the cab midway over the boiler and ahead of the firebox. A telephone kept engineer and fireman in touch. Their class name of Atlantic was, of course, adopted for all locomotives with the 4-4-2 wheel arrangement.

Large Atlantics were built by the American Locomotive Co after 1904. They had tapered boilers, outside cylinders and worked at 200 pounds pressure. Known as the *Big Four* class, they ran on the Cleveland, Cincinatti, Chicago and St Louis tracks.

The first American 4-6-2 was built in 1901 for New Zealand and given the name *Pacific,* also to become the wheel classification description for all such engines. On tests prior to export its performance was so impressive that United States railroads asked for similar designs which could be used both for heavy freight and fast expresses. In 1904 Baldwins produced what they claimed to be the largest and heaviest locomotive in the world, a 160-ton Pacific for the Union Pacific. It was powered by two outside cylinders of 22 by 28 inches driving coupled wheels of 6 feet 5 inches.

With fast, workmanlike engines of these types the United States could emulate the high speed of expresses

The ultimate in big steam locomotives in the closing years of the steam era: Union Pacific's *Big Boy* articulated 4-8-8-4s were introduced in 1941 to handle heavy freight as American industrial production was geared to a war situation. They were a larger version of the *Challenger* class of 4-6-6-4s, which began operating five years earlier.

below At the turn of the century the ubiquitous 4-4-0 of American railroads began to give way to heavier engines capable of hauling longer trains at higher speeds. This photo shows Northern Pacific's *North Coast Limited* hauled by a 4-6-0 on its maiden trip in April, 1900.

bottom The idea of an articulated locomotive originated in America in 1831 when Horatio Allen joined two engines back to back with one boiler and firebox. The first American compound using the Mallet system was designed by J. E. Muhlfeld of the Baltimore and Ohio Railroad in conjunction with the American Locomotive Co. The engine was affectionately known as 'Old Maud'.

opposite page A 4-6-2 Pacific-type locomotive of the Illinois Central Railroad.

in Britain and Europe. With their freight locomotives, American engineers surpassed anything built elsewhere. In 1882 The Southern Pacific Railroad experimented with *Mastodon,* a 4-10-0; it was successful as regards tractive effort, but was so greedy for steam that its firebox was hopelessly inadequate. This defect was remedied by modifying the design in the *Santa Fe* class of 2-10-2s, the trailing pair of wheels carrying a larger firebox. Built by Baldwins in 1903, they were four-cylinder compounds and weighed 200 tons. With a starting tractive effort of 69,500 pounds they were the most powerful engines in existence, and replaced two and even three engines when hauling freight through mountainous country on the Atchison, Topeka and Santa Fe lines.

In 1897 Japan had asked Baldwins to design a freight engine to augment the 4-6-0 outside cylinder locomotives they were using on their British-built line from Tokyo to Yokohama. Baldwin's built a 2-8-2 which they named *Mikado.* (This, of course, became the descriptive name for all 2-8-2s, except for a brief interval in 1942 when sensitive United States managements re-named the type *McArthur*). Rapidly *Mikados* appeared on all major United States railroads, and for a generation were the most numerous freight engines in service, partly because in 1918 the Federal administration specified the *Mikado* as an authorized design for war-time construction. In that year alone some 900 were built.

Another special order for export which quickly went into domestic use was the compound articulated engine based on the design introduced by Anatole Mallet in

1876. Originally these engines were wanted for badly laid and tortuous lines, with severe gradients and violent curves. Most were built for narrow gauge lines and were quite light. American designers increased the scale. At the St Louis Exposition of 1904 the American Locomotive Co exhibited a Mallet 0-6-6-0 ordered by the Baltimore and Ohio Railroad. The driving wheels of 4 feet 8 inches shared the weight of the 21-foot boiler. Low pressure cylinders powered the forward group of drivers, and high pressure cylinders the rear group. Apart from impressing the public with its size, this engine at first created little interest among railroad managements. But two years later the Great Northern ordered five Mallets, and their obvious success stimulated orders by every United States line carrying heavy freight.

The giant of all such engines was built by Baldwins for the Erie Railroad. This was a Triplex Mallet with a 2-8-8-8-2 wheel arrangement. Three were in service by 1913. The engine was capable of hauling a load of 15,300 tons, and a sight of those days unlikely ever to be repeated was an Erie freight train four miles in length.

Mallets have the distinction of being the most tenacious opponents of the diesel in the United States. The Union Pacific's *Challenger* class of 4-6-6-4s, first built in 1936, and its *Big Boy* 4-8-8-4s introduced in 1941, hauled UP's freight trains until the late 1950s, when steam locomotives were becoming a curiosity in a land of diesels, automobiles and aircraft.

While the United States favoured the Mallet type of articulated locomotive, in the British Empire the most widely used was the Beyer-Garratt, patented by

right *King's Canterbury,* **one of Southern Railway's** *Schools* **class. These 4-4-0s were designed by R. E. L. Maunsell in 1930, primarily for operation on gradients and severe curves of the London-Hastings line. They proved so successful that they were soon working expresses to the Portsmouth, Southampton, and Bournemouth area. They are regarded as the finest 4-4-0s ever built in Britain.**

bottom *The Red Knight,* **one of Maunsell's** *King Arthur* **class, the first of which was built in 1925.**

an Australian inventor, H. W. Garratt in 1907. In the Garratt design the boiler is carried on a girder frame, pivoted and supported at each end by bogies and the driving wheels. Thus two power units were served by one steam source. The first to operate was an 0-4-0+ 0-4-0 on the narrow gauge Tasmanian Railway. After Beyer, Peacock acquired the patents, very powerful Garratts were built both before and after the First World War. Every line in British-controlled Africa had them, and they worked Indian trains in the Himalayan foothills.

The usual wheel arrangement was 2-6-2+2-6-2 with six cylinders. Their most spectacular work was on the notorious Rimutaka section in New Zealand, which possessed eighty major curves over a distance of seventeen miles, and gradients of up to 1:15. Previously two to four engines had been needed; the Garratts worked solo.

Despite the fact that Britain produced Garratts in quantity for overseas lines, none was used in the United Kingdom until 1925, when one 2-8-0+0-8-2 was built for the LNER for mineral trains in South Yorkshire. Two years later the LMS ordered some 2-6-0+0-6-2s to handle coal trains from the Midlands to the London area.

The restriction of export trade through the pressures of war forced Britain's traditional customers to fend for themselves. Australia started her own locomotive shops in Sydney under government control. The first built there was a 4-6-4 tanker, *No 1063,* soon followed by a series of United States-style superheater 2-8-0s. But the most impressive were the three-cylinder 4-8-2s built after 1918. They were required for hauling the heavy freight and passenger trains on the 402-mile route from Sydney to the border of Victoria. A feature of these engines was the mechanical stoker.

Canada had for long relied almost entirely on the United States for locomotives. But prior to 1914 Canadian Pacific operated two-cylinder compound 4-6-0s, which were built by the North British Locomotive Co to a Canadian design. Their rivals were the outside cylinder 4-6-0s, built by the American Locomotive Co for the Grand Trunk Railroad. These engines hauled the *International Limited* on the 841-mile run between Montreal and Chicago.

During 1914–18 the shortage of locomotives became worldwide. By 1916, although not at war, the United States was hard-pressed to find adequate rolling stock for booming industry. As soon as the United States entered the war engines were shipped in quantity to Britain and France, most of the 3,400 United States locomotives built in 1917 going overseas or being held in reserve for any spreading of hostilities.

In Britain the railways' resources were stretched beyond reasonable limits. Internal services for moving troops and munitions were the heaviest ever, while freight engines had to be sent to the war zones of France, Italy, and the Middle East.

108

A bizarre incident of wartime railway operation in the United Kingdom was the presence of some German locomotives on the SE & CR. These handy 4-4-0s, from the Berlin firm of Borsig, had been ordered in January 1914 by R. E. Maunsell, ostensibly for the forthcoming summer holiday traffic to the Thanet resorts, but probably as the result of a discreet hint from the government that the Kent lines might be very busy before the year was out. The contract stipulated delivery of ten engines by June. They arrived unassembled towards the end of May, accompanied by German fitters who were working at Ashford until three weeks before war broke out.

Maunsell supplemented these engines with his famous N class of 2-6-0 mixed traffic locomotives, with 19 by 28-inch cylinders and driving wheels of 5½ feet. Winston Churchill, then Minister of Munitions, envisaged civilian employment problems when the war ended and the munition plants closed down. He authorized schemes for alternative work. At Woolwich Arsenal production began in 1919 of the Maunsell engines, almost inevitably dubbed 'Woolworths' on account of their place of origin and their utility design, bereft of all frills. These workmanlike engines operated on railways both in this country and Europe, and the basic design was adopted on the Southern for light expresses and fast freight trains until 1945.

The war frustrated the ambitious plans for the GNR drawn up by the line's new locomotive chief, Herbert N. (later Sir Nigel) Gresley, who took over at Doncaster in 1912 on Ivatt's retirement. Gresley was, during the war years and the immediate aftermath, young enough to ignore the allegations of near-failure in 1908 of the GWR *Great Bear,* which had created an unwarranted suspicion about the value of Pacifics. The first GNR 4-6-2, *No 1470 Great Northern,* steamed out of the Doncaster yard in 1922, with Gresley's confident assurance that it would handle trains of 550 to 600 tons on schedules drawn up for expresses of half the weight. These magnificent engines had three cylinders of 20 by 26 inches, all driving the middle coupled axle. Boiler pressure was raised to 220 pounds and the cylinder diameter reduced to 19 inches.

On 1 January 1923 Britain's railways were amalgamated in four groups. Within days of the GNR becoming absorbed in the LNER the most famous of the Gresley Pacifics was ready: *No 1472 Flying Scotsman* (later renumbered *4472*). Four years later, a gentlemanly version of the 'Race to the North' was resumed by the LMS and LNER. Gresley's first gesture was to announce an express non-stop from London to Newcastle, first run by *Flying Fox.* The LMS replied by running non-stop from London to Carlisle. Gresley, in conditions of secrecy, built tenders with a corridor passage so that crews could change over without stopping, and in 1928 there began a regular non-stop run of 392·7 miles from King's Cross to Edinburgh.

Record-breaking by *Flying Scotsman* was not over. On 30 November 1934, with a special four-coach train, *No 4472* reached 100 mph, authenticated in the dynamometer car. Other records made on that memorable day included an average of 80 mph for 250 miles and 90 mph for 40 miles. The 100 mph record was broken seven years later, when on 5 March 1935 Gresley's improved Pacific, *Papyrus,* reached 108 mph.

The culmination of the Gresley Pacific design came in the *A4* class originally intended for the Silver Jubilee express service of 1935. Cylinder diameter was reduced to 18½ inches and steam pressure increased to 250 pounds. The first engine of this class, *Silver Link,* was streamlined, not as was alleged as a publicity gimmick, but as a result of wind tunnel tests. On a demonstration run from King's Cross to Grantham and back *Silver*

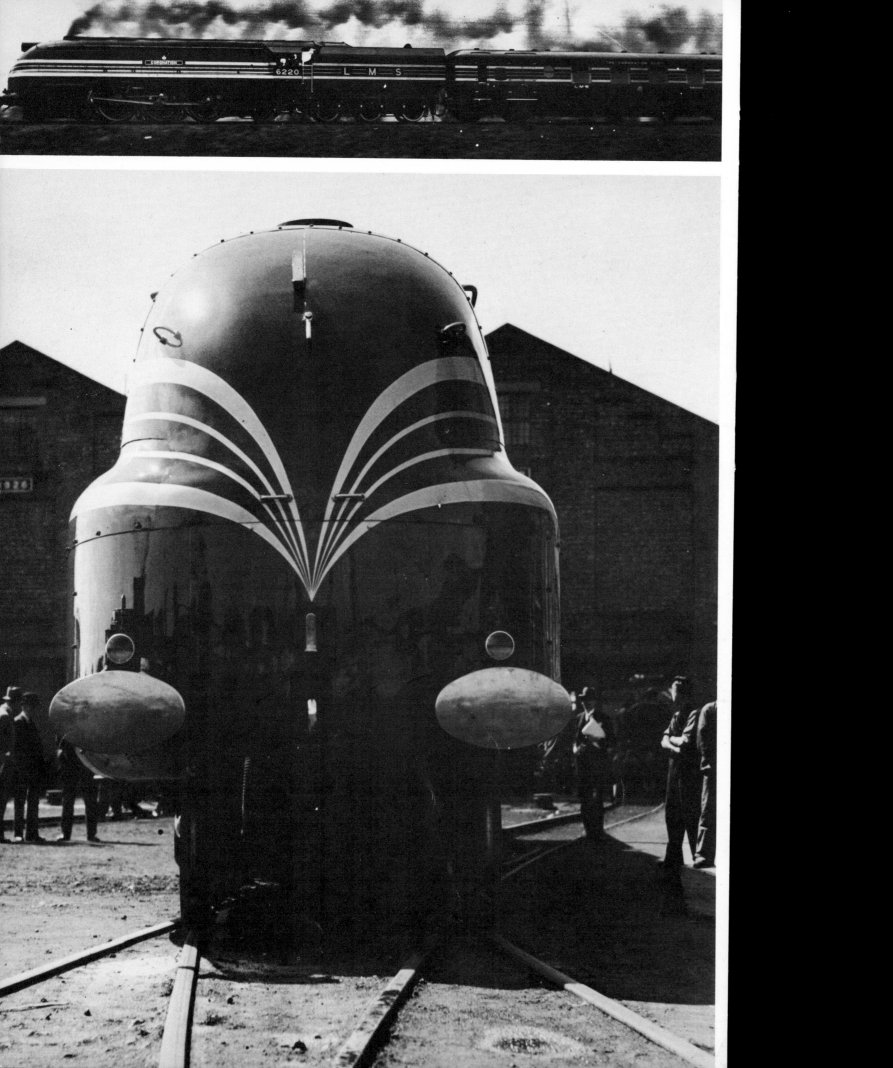

opposite, top *Coronation Scot* **at speed near King's Langley, Hertfordshire in 1939. Five engines of this class were built to mark the coronation of George VI. On a trial run this Pacific reached 114 mph and averaged 79·7 mph over the 158 miles from Crewe to London.** *Coronation* **was exhibited at the 1939 New York World's Fair.**

opposite, bottom **The modernistic 'face' of** *Coronation.* **On normal express service the engine was painted in Prussian Blue with silver-white embellishments, but for its American exhibition the colour was changed to the traditional Derby Red of the LMS.**

below *Sir Nigel Gresley,* **a restored** *A4* **class locomotive. Perhaps the most famous of these Pacific-types was** *Mallard,* **holder of the world record for a steam locomotive at 126 mph.**

opposite, top A *Jubilee* class 4-6-0, *No 45562 Alberta,* climbing Shap en route from Bradford to Carlisle. A total of 190 of these Stanier locomotives were built from 1935 onwards, marking George V's silver jubilee and named after regions of the British Commonwealth.

opposite, bottom A Stanier *Black Five* 4-6-0 with a freight train near Tebay, Westmorland. First introduced in 1934, there were eventually 842 of these useful engines on British Railways.

below *No 4073 Caerphilly Castle* was the first of its class, built in 1923. C. B. Collett's design of this four cylinder 4-6-0 was so much in advance of its period that it was used, with minor changes, for Swindon engines until 1950. Record after record, including a top speed of 100 mph, were made by *Castle* locomotives.

bottom The photo of *Chepstow Castle* was taken in July, 1926. The GWR, always alert for publicity, organized formal visits of the *Castle* engines to the towns after which they were named, with invitations to local notabilities to inspect their 'own locomotive'.

Link touched 112 mph. With the second engine of the class, *Quicksilver,* a daily service between London and Newcastle was maintained at an average of 67 mph. To complete the triumphant story of the Gresley Pacifics, in June 1938 *No 4468 Mallard* achieved the world record speed for a steam locomotive, 126 mph.

The LMS, LNER's contestant for the lucrative Anglo-Scottish traffic, relied in the first period of grouping on a design originating on the Midland in 1902: the Johnson 4-4-0 three-cylinder compound. Over the years it had been steadily improved, emerging as one of the most successful classes of this century. Richard Deeley took Johnson's original design, and in 1905 built a modified version, with simpler controls of the variation in the admission of steam to the high and low pressure cylinders, and with pressure increased to 220 pounds. In 1913, when these engines were sent to Derby for a major refit, they were rebuilt as superheaters by Henry Fowler, who succeeded Deeley in 1909.

Although the LMS selected the Deeley-Fowler compounds as a standard, with forty built in 1924 (followed by a further 195), they were too light for the heavy West Coast expresses of the inter-war years. In 1927 Fowler, in co-operation with the North British Locomotive Co, produced the 4-6-0 *Royal Scot* class. They were simple engines with 18 by 26-inch cylinders working at a steam pressure of 250 pounds. Although design and production were rushed through to meet a traffic crisis, the class was an unqualified success. Fifty were built, twenty-five named after Scottish regiments and the rest reviving such historic locomotive names as *Lancashire Witch.*

In 1930 Sir Henry Fowler retired. His post was given to W. A. (later Sir William) Stanier, who had hitherto been with the GWR at Swindon. The result was a tacit challenge to the LNER with faster expresses, given such names as Manchester Flyer and Liverpool Flyer, with improved engines of the *Royal Scot* class.

In 1934 Stanier introduced the Class 5 of 4-6-0s known as *Black Five* because of their black livery denoting a mixed traffic engine. Rarely has there been a more versatile locomotive, capable of handling the heaviest freight trains or topping 85 mph with expresses. The *Black Fives* were turned out year after year until, in 1951, in the evening of the steam engine day, 842 had been built.

Of greater impact on the public was the Stanier Pacific brought out in 1933–the *Princess* class strongly reminiscent of *Great Bear* and with touches of the GWR *Kings.* These four-cylinder engines with divided drive were designed to take heavy expresses between London and Glasgow. The first, *Princess Royal,* was in the nature of an experimental prototype, and after trials the boiler design was modified. The first record breaker in this class was *Princess Elizabeth,* which on 16 November 1936 averaged 68 mph non-stop from Euston to Glasgow, and next day did the return trip at an average of 70 mph.

A unique engine in this class was *No 6202,* which

began life in 1926 as an experimental turbine loco-motive. The design of the Swedish engineer Fredrik Ljungström was used, adopting the turbine arrange-ment of the 0-6-4s operated successfully in Sweden since 1921. The LMS turbine cruised smoothly at 75 mph, and savings on coal and water were impressive. After years of service the engine was rebuilt as a *Princess*. It was one of the locomotives involved in the rail disaster of 1952 at Harrow and Wealdstone station.

The 'Lizzies', as they were affectionately known, were followed by Stanier's streamlined Pacific in all-blue livery, *Coronation*. On a demonstration run with the Coronation Scot express a speed of 114 mph was attained.

Resourceful public relations, backed by spectacular record breaking, focussed the limelight on the two railways linking Scotland and the North with London. Comparatively quietly the GWR went about enhancing its reputation as a fast, reliable line. Its splendid passenger services during the inter-war years were founded on the 4-6-0 four-cylinder *Castle* class, intro-duced in 1923 by C. B. Collett and built until 1950 in a series of improved versions.

Collett used many of the features of the GWR *Stars*. Cylinder diameter was increased to 16 inches and the boiler heating surface was 2,049 square feet. The first of these fine engines was *Caerphilly Castle*, used in exchange trials with a LNER Gresley Pacific in 1925. The smaller *Castle* proved equal in performance to the LNER engine, and was an easy victor on economy of

fuel consumption. Records by the *Castles* include an average of 81·6 mph from Swindon to Paddington by *Tregenna Castle* in 1932 and 100 mph by *Builth Castle* on the Honeybourne bank in the Vale of Evesham.

Four years after the first *Castle* Collett produced a heavier version: the *King* class. These were nominally the most powerful 4-6-0 passenger engines ever made in Britain and were built to handle heavy expresses on the gradient around and west of Exeter. The first of the class to be built, *King George V,* was almost immediately shipped to the United States to take part in the 'Fair of the Iron Horse' marking the centenary of the Balti-more and Ohio Railroad.

Collett achieved another success in 1928 when he replaced the old GWR 4-4-0s with the *Hall* class of two-cylinder 4-6-0s for mixed traffic. Their names almost exceeded the number of England's stately homes, 330 being built at Swindon.

On the fourth railway under the 1923 grouping, the Southern, Maunsell first took the two-cylinder 4-6-0s of the old LSWR, and made modifications in the design. To help in advertising the attractions of the legendary West Country the SR publicity department suggested these engines were named after the Knights of the Round Table. They proved so successful that all sorts of names connected with the Arthurian legend had to be used, with the result that overseas visitors from both United States and Europe were charmed to find their boat trains were engined by *Maid of Astolat, Merlin, Excalibur,* and so on.

below *Sir Walter Raleigh,* **one of the** *Lord Nelson* **class for the Southern Railway. These locomotives were designed to give the power needed for a schedule of express services averaging 50 mph with up to 500 tons of rolling stock. The first was in operation in 1926; all were named after famous naval commanders.**

right **A Bulleid Pacific-type engine of the** *Merchant Navy* **class. The first one appeared in 1941, its remarkable appearance causing consternation among amateur traditionalists.**

Maunsell was impressed by the GWR *Castles,* as indeed was every railway engineer in Britain and overseas. He thereupon designed the *Lord Nelson* class. This 4-6-0 had four high pressure cylinders of $16\frac{1}{2}$ by 26 inches. An innovation was setting the cranks of the inside and outside cylinders at 45 degrees with one another. With a tractive effort of 33,510 pounds at 85 per cent of steam pressure *Lord Nelson* was an unqualified success from the time of its introduction in 1926.

As well as its long routes to the South-West the SR had to service the short and difficult lines in Kent and Sussex. For these Maunsell produced in 1930 another locomotive unsurpassed in its class: 4-4-0. This three-cylinder engine was a hybrid of the *King Arthur* and *Nelson* designs, using a short version of the former's boiler and the cylinders and valve gear of the latter. To the delight of young railway enthusiasts they were named after English public schools. *No 900 Eton* was the first in regular service.

Maunsell was succeeded in 1938 by O. V. S. Bulleid, taking charge of steam motive power at a time when the Southern was extending its electrification. However, with war imminent it was clear that major permanent way changes would be impossible, though freight and passenger traffic would be on a wartime scale. *Channel Packet,* the first of Bulleid's *Merchant Navy* class Pacifics, was built during wartime, with official approval, in order to maintain services. These were fast, powerful engines with three cylinders of 18 by 24 inches. Boiler pressure was 280 pounds. The enclosed valve gear was Bulleid's own invention. To the onlooker the striking features were the streamlined casing and the American-style slotted wheels.

At the end of the war a lighter version of the *Merchant Navies* appeared, two series named after places served by the old LSWR and a third, the *Battle of Britain* class, to commemorate Britain's 'finest hour' in 1940. After nationalization the streamlined casing was removed from these stalwarts of the SR's express services and boat trains.

HONOURABLE FINALE

In the years between the wars the worldwide trend was towards standardization. Not only the steam engine, but the railway on which it ran, was being seriously challenged by the internal combustion engine on the road and in the air. Rationalization had to be the watchword in fact of the new competition.

In 1920 the United States had some 60,000 engines operating. Yet over the entire country there were under a hundred different types, and almost half of these were no longer being made.

Standardization reached its peak in the newly-born Soviet Union. In 1920, after studying American and German designs, the Russian engineers designed their Class *E* 0-10-0 freight engines. Orders for the parts were distributed among twenty German and Swedish firms, and so precise were the blueprints supplied from Moscow that assembly presented no problem. Many hundreds of these engines were built. They were followed by the *FD* class of 2-10-2s, built in Russia and based closely on American design. A passenger version of this engine, a 2-8-4, the *Josef Stalin* class, appeared in 1930. Four years later what was claimed to be the most powerful engine ever built, a 2-14-4, worked with freight in the Urals. Evidently it was not a success for only two were built.

Soviet locomotive stocks were virtually wiped out during the Second World War, either by lack of maintenance or enemy destruction. The shortage was met with 2,000 engines supplied by Britain and the United States and as reparations, mostly from Germany and Hungary. These engines were carefully tested and, in many cases, stripped and their metals analyzed. The outcome was a standard general purpose engine, the *L* class 2-10-0. This was produced in quantity until 1954, when it was replaced by the *LV* 2-10-2 class. Noteworthy was the adaptability of their fuel systems, and different types within the class burned coal dust, liquefied gas, and oil. They were the last Russian steam engines to be built. In 1955 Russia aimed to eliminate steam by 1970. As with most plans, the deadline had to be deferred. Steam remains a force on Soviet lines.

In Britain the postwar period saw the *Liberation* 2-8-0's tackling the problems of restoring peacetime services. These engines, built for the Ministry of Supply during the war to a design by R. A. Riddles, seconded from the LMS, were austere and stripped of all frills. More than 700 ran on British rails after 1945, and scores were sent to liberated Europe.

They were augmented by the class of Pacifics usually known as *Britannia,* the first new design of the nationalized British railway system, and by the *BR*5 class of 4-6-0s. By then it was known that the steam engine in Britain would soon disappear. In 1955 the order went out to phase out steam. In the United States the decision had already been made. No steam locomotive was bought by American railroads after 1953. By 1967 only twenty-one steam engines were listed as

Union Pacific's 4-6-6-4 *Challenger* class, the first of a type
built in 1936 for freight and passenger service.

operational on any United States public transportation system. The machine which had helped to create a unified nation was relegated to museums and amusement parks.

In Britain, home of the steam engine, the last locomotive to be built was a class of 2-10-0s. With a nice sense of history the Swindon engineers changed the standard black livery of British Rail to a handsome green on the last of the class to be built in 1960: *No 92220*. When it steamed out on the time-honoured route of the old GWR it bore the name, *Evening Star*. One hundred and twenty years before, *Morning Star* had inaugurated travel on the same track. The story of the steam locomotive was completed.

opposite page **British Railways heavy 2-10-0 freight locomotive built at Crewe in 1955. Ten of these engines were built for handling mineral traffic. They had Franco-Crost boilers and intrigued the public because the smoke was dispersed through a side vent just ahead of the cab window.**

below **A French 2-8-2 locomotive of the** *141 P* **class, with internal and external streamlining, which operated on French railways right up to the 1960s.**

bottom *Braunton,* **a Bulleid Pacific, leaving Bournemouth Central for London in August, 1965. These 'West Country' engines were a lighter version of the Southern's** *Merchant Navy* **class; they were followed by a batch named after personalities of the Battle of Britain, and then a further series of 'West Country' names. After 1957 several of them were rebuilt.**

A German *DB* 2-10-0 class *44 No 463* hauling a Horb-Rottwell
freight out of a tunnel near Oberndorff.

A class *94* 2-10-0 *No 92076* climbing Shap at Scout Green on a
dawn freight, banked by a tank locomotive at the rear.

INDEX

127

ACKNOWLEDGMENTS:

Colour

Alpha, New York 31(B), 83;
British Rail 56–57; H. P. Bulmer
Limited 22; Derek Cross 26, 53,
113; Frank Dumbleton 61(T),
64(B); Hamlyn Group Library;
Derek Huntriss 31(T), 49(T),
86(B), 87(B), 91, 94–95, 116, 117;
Robin Lush 30, 60, 61(B), 86(T),
90(T), 125, and front and back
jackets; John S. Whiteley 23,
27, 49(B), 52, 64(T), 87(T), 124;

Black and white

Ian Allan Limited 84(T), 85(B);
Association of American
Railroads 36–37(T), 72(B), 73;
Alan L. Bailey 102(TL);
Baltimore & Ohio Railroad
Company 35, 39(T), 39(B), 76,
106(B); British Rail 54, 65(T),
68(T), 79(T), 79(B), 81(T), 90(B),
109(T), 109(B), 118(TL);
British Transport Commission
(Historic Relics) 85(T);

Canadian Pacific 77(T); Fox
Photos 46–47, 111(B), 112(T),
112(B), 119; French Railways
Limited 58(B), 123(T); John R.
Hume 96; D. A. Idle 84(B),
111(T); Illinois Central
Railroad 41, 107; Keystone
Press Agency 122;
Lichtbildstelle Der
Bunderbarndirektion, Nurnberg
99B; London Transport Board
62–63, 66(B); The Mansell
Collection 44; Mary Evans
Picture Library 88–89, 93(TR);
Museum of British Transport
59(T); Museon Di Rodo 92(T),
92(B); Museum of Science &
Industry 77(B); New South
Wales Government Office,
London 66(T); New Zealand
Railways 68(B) 100(T); Northern
Pacific Railway 106(T); Penn

Central Transportation
Company 37(B); Pennsylvania
Railroad 32–33; Ivo Peters
114(B); Radio Times Hulton
Picture Library 12, 24, 74(T),
100(B), 115(T), 115(B); Railway
Museum, Swindon 45(T); P.
Ransome-Wallis 81(B); Real
Photographs Company Limited
80(C), 80(B); The Science
Museum, London 6–7, 8–9, 10,
11, 13(T), 13(B), 14, 15(T), 15(B),
16, 17, 21, 25, 28(T), 28(B), 29, 34,
38(T), 38(C), 40, 42–43, 45(B),
50–51, 55(T), 55(C), 55(B), 58(T),
59(B), 65(C), 67, 72(T), 99(T),
99(C), 102–103(B); Southern
Pacific Company 74(B), 75;
Ullstein Bilderdienst 48; Union
Pacific Railroad 38(B), 70–71,
104–105, 121; John S. Whiteley
114(T), 123(B).